Rooted
Woman of Valor

By Jan C Thompson

Hi Tara,

It was a delight to meet you on our Israel trip. Here is the book I wrote last year Rooted in the Old Testament chapter of Proverbs 31. May the journey into her "Fear of God" heart encourage your walk with the Lord. Blessings, Jan C Thompson

Copyright Notice

Cover and interior design: Derick Gentry Thompson
Cover and interior art and calligraphy: Gloria Seitz

Email: jancthompson@gmail.com
Website/blog: http://jancthompson.com/
Library of Congress Cataloging-in-publication Data

Thompson, Jan C
Rooted Woman of Valor/Jan C Thompson

ISBN 978-1-548765-97-2

Acknowledgements

When I first taught the concepts of this book at retreats, Rick and I were young parents of David, Derick, and Tiffany. Now several decades later, the whole family joined my book team as skilled writers, designers, editors, and prayerful cheerleaders. I cherish each of them! They graciously offered some of their creative prose and lyrics that speak beautifully to different parts of the book.

The lovely watercolor scene on the book cover, inside art, and calligraphy were painted by a ministry friend, Gloria Seitz. As a woman of valor, she offered her generous gift of art to enrich my words. Thank you, Gloria!

I am eternally grateful for many ministry women who modeled for me what it means to live on this earth as a woman of valor. Some have joined the heavenly cloud of witnesses. Early on, my mother, Dorothy, challenged me to minister to others through my gifts. Mrs. Eastep, my childhood pastor's wife, and mentor nurtured my love for reading, studying, and writing God's truths.

Thank you to my daughter-in-laws, Beth and Michelle, and our grandchildren, who add delight to our extended family. Finally, what a privilege it is to have my sister, Kim Gromacki, as a lifelong encourager toward becoming a woman of valor!

Gratefully,

Jan C Thompson

Dedication

To my Lord and Savior,
Who creates a woman of valor

To my husband of valor,
Richard Gentry Thompson

To my children of valor,
David, Derick and Tiffany Thompson

Contents

Introduction

During my single years into marriage, God blessed me with godly and rooted women for role models. Each of them invested their time and treasure into my soul's refinement. Their faces line my heart like a portrait gallery of women of valor. Watching their courageous actions and attitudes painted bold strokes of bravery and strength of character on my heart. From my mother-in-law, Ruth, and childhood pastor's wife, Mrs. Eastep, who became young widows, to others facing life-threatening illnesses or difficult family challenges, each adorns a medal of valor.

Grateful for their impact, I realized after the honeymoon of marriage and ministry, that it was essential that I dig into the Scriptures to give the Master painter the needed time and attention to develop His portrait of me. I longed to become a fruitful woman in my home, ministry, and world. I was aware of potential weeds inside myself and the world around me. Years went by, and pressures increased. Some seemed entangling and even strangling my prayer to live the flourishing life envisioned in the Scriptures and by my women of valor.

Colossians 1:9-12 embodied my heart's prayer and those of my mentors.
"For this reason, since the day we heard about you, we have not stopped praying for you. We continually ask God to fill you with the knowledge of His will through all the wisdom and understanding that the Spirit gives, so that you may live a life worthy of the Lord and please Him in every way: bearing fruit in every good work, growing in the knowledge of God, being strengthened with all power according to His glorious might so that you may have great endurance and patience, and giving joyful thanks to the Father, who has qualified you to share in the inheritance of His holy people in the kingdom of light." (NIV)

My passion for grow in fruitfulness led me to a personal study of the book of Proverbs to gather wise insights from its pages. Arriving at the last, but not least chapter, Proverbs 31, I knew I needed to spend extended time gazing at the portrait our Lord painted of this fruitful woman.

My previous quick glances at this superwoman made me feel a bit overwhelmed. At the beginning of my in-depth study, I was the mother of three young children. The velocity of the twenty-two verses of this woman's life reminded me of our busy days. The bright fruit of her actions colored by her attitudes caught my attention. The enduring impact for me came on a reflective journey with this fruitful woman as my mentor and friend. The portrait of her life began to emerge into a sturdy, beautiful tree. The fruit of her life, the anchoring roots, and the resources that nurture her developed a new vision for the upcoming decades of my life's journey.

Backstory of the Woman of Valor

Long ago in a land far away, there was a queen mother who prayed for her son to become a wise king, husband, and father. She offered an inspired saying that her son wrote down in the last chapter of the book of Proverbs. The insightful words for her son included a manhood challenge and a poem that painted the portrait of the wife he should seek.

As a wise mother, her first words were to challenge him to become a man worthy of a godly wife, and a king ready to lead his people. She calls him to three essential leadership principles in Proverbs 31:2-9 (NIV).

The Challenge to become a worthy King, Husband, and Father

- **Listen** to wisdom.
  "Listen, my son! Listen, son of my womb!
  Listen, my son, answer to my prayers!" (31:2)

- **Learn** to apply wisdom's insights on how leaders
  should live a life of valor and strength. (31:4-7)

- **Lead** others by speaking up, judging fairly,
  and defending the needy. (31:8,9)

With beauty and grace, this mother continues by penning a prophetic poem that paints the portrait of the woman her royal son should seek for his wife. She begins with the inspired question,

---

Who can find an aishes chayil (woman of valor, an excellent wife)?

Proverbs 31:10 (Orthodox Jewish Bible)

The Hebrew language translates, **aishes chayil,** as the woman of valor. There is a Hebrew tradition for the men of the family to read or sing Proverbs 31:10-31 at the beginning of the Friday night sabbath to express honor and appreciation for all the women of the family.

The format of Proverbs 31:10-31 is twenty-two verses beginning consecutively with the Hebrew alphabet. This portrait of the woman of valor embodies wisdom from A to Z! An acrostic poem seeks to provide a sense of completeness, as well as ease in remembering. (At the end of this section, I created an English acrostic version based on the ESV Bible that helped me memorize its truths.)

Now 3,000 years later these inspired words continue to be treasured as a masterpiece. As we take the time to reflect on the portrait of this Rooted Woman of Valor, it brings to mind a scene in one of C.S. Lewis' ***Chronicle of Narnia*** series. In the third book called, ***The Voyage of the Dawn Treader***, Lucy, Edmund, and Eustice notice a painting of a beautiful ocean vessel. Suddenly, they find themselves becoming part of the canvas. Afloat on a mighty ship, no longer at their home, they are heading toward a great adventure.

Let us enter the Proverbs 31 world and meet the woman of valor face to face. As our fruitful mentor and guide, she will lead us toward the adventure God created for us. Jumping into the portrait begins by reading the inspired verses of this masterpiece.

Portrait of a Rooted Woman of Valor

Proverbs 31:10-31

10 An excellent wife (woman of valor) who can find?
She is far more precious than jewels.

11 The heart of her husband trusts in her,
and he will have no lack of gain.

12 She does him good, and not harm,
all the days of her life.

13 She seeks wool and flax,
and works with willing hands.

14 She is like the ships of the merchant;
she brings her food from afar.

15 She rises while it is yet night
and provides food for her household
and portions for her maidens.

16 She considers a field and buys it;
with the fruit of her hands she plants a vineyard.

17 She dresses herself with strength
and makes her arms strong.

18 She perceives that her merchandise is profitable.
Her lamp does not go out at night.

19 She puts her hands to the distaff,
and her hands hold the spindle.

20 She opens her hand to the poor
and reaches out her hands to the needy.

21 She is not afraid of snow for her household,
for all her household are clothed in scarlet.

22 She makes bed coverings for herself;
her clothing is fine linen and purple.

23 Her husband is known in the gates
when he sits among the elders of the land.

24 She makes linen garments and sells them;
she delivers sashes to the merchant.

25 Strength and dignity are her clothing,
and she laughs at the time to come.

26 She opens her mouth with wisdom,
and the teaching of kindness is on her tongue.

27 She looks well to the ways of her household
and does not eat the bread of idleness.

28 Her children rise up and call her blessed;
her husband also, and he praises her:

29 "Many women have done excellently,
but you surpass them all."

30 Charm is deceitful, and beauty is vain,
but a woman who fears the Lord is to be praised.

31 Give her of the fruit of her hands,
and let her works praise her in the gates.

Our portrait of the inspired Proverbs 31

Rooted Woman of Valor

is painted in three primary factors

of a vibrant tree as presented in

Jeremiah 17:8.

"He (she) is like a tree planted by water,

that sends its roots by the stream,

and does not fear when the heat comes,

for its leaves remain green,

and is not anxious in the year of drought

for it does not cease to bear fruit."

- **Fruit Factor of Woman of Valor**

- **Root Factor of Woman of Valor**

- **Soil Factor of Woman of Valor**

Fruit Factor

of the

Woman of Valor

All portraits have the goal of creating a picture that shapes the essential qualities of the person. As we gaze at our Proverbs 31 mentor, she is like a tree laden with fruit that encapsulates her life's journey.

HER TITLE

A woman of valor, an excellent wife who can find? (31:10a OJB)

Our introduction to our Proverbs 31 woman comes encased in a question. The king's mother wants him to begin his quest for his future wife with a specific vision in mind. Her inspired title focuses on her valor and excellence. The definition of **Valor** (chayil) is to be brave, strong, resourceful, and powerful. **Excellent** is to have outstanding qualities and remarkable goodness.

We will discover the portrait of this woman has the primary brushstrokes on her heart, soul, and mind. Valor and excellence adorn her life shaped by her actions and attitudes. Blended with her title is the description of her worth.

HER WORTH

She is far more precious than jewels. (31:10b)

What beautiful words to express the value of a woman's life! She is considered more precious than jewels or expensive gifts. As we look at her specific life realms, they may not seem spectacular enough to warrant such value. Without fanfare, it is in the convergence of her actions and attitudes where such beauty and value grow to impact her world.

Her precious value shines forth from the fruit she bears in the various realms of her life. This rooted woman of valor has **Five Life Realms** where her strengths are evident from Proverbs 31:11-29.

1. Marriage
2. Home & Work
3. World
4. Character
5. Rewards

Fruit in Her Life Realms

1. HER MARRIAGE

Fruit of Trustworthy Love

**The heart of her husband trusts in her,
and he will have no lack of gain. (31:11)**

First and foremost, this woman has a trustworthy relationship with her husband, as well as family, friends, and coworkers. His heart trusts her with settled confidence that removes the question about what she does with her time, their money, resources, and training of children. He knows she is committed to him and their family, because of her personal goal to have "a pure heart and a good conscience and a sincere faith" (I Timothy 1:5 NIV).

As we journey through her days, we will see our mentor's trustworthy marriage enriches all aspects of her life. With their marital bond before God as the foundation, she carefully nurtures mutual trust by her actions and attitudes

Trustworthy Love's Action is
to bring her husband good, not harm
She does him good, and not harm, (31:12a)

With a heart committed to their marriage, our woman of valor focuses her actions toward bringing good and not harm to her husband. Her moral compass nurtures a pure heart, good conscience, and sincere faith as she pursues the goal of love toward her husband and everyone in her world. The wisdom of Scripture draws her into a lifestyle that brings relational fulfillment and peace.

A single woman's Trustworthy Love grows as she relates to her parents, friends and all she meets. II Timothy 2:22 provides a compass, "Flee the evil desires of youth and pursue righteousness, faith, love, and peace, along with those who call on the Lord out of a pure heart." (NIV)

Trustworthy Love's Attitude is
rooted in her marriage covenant
all the days of her life. (31:12b)

"All the days of her life" captures her attitude toward her husband. Based on their marital covenant before their God, their love seeks to weather the good and bad during the early springtime of young affection on through their retirement years. Of course, there are days when she will not like her husband's actions or her reactions. Whether once a year, month, or week, she renews her attitudes and actions toward her marital covenant. Her promise 'in sickness and health, to love and to cherish, until death us do part,' guides her heart to find reliable solutions to grow a rooted love with her husband "all the days of her life."

In so few words, so much lived! This lifelong trust takes strength beyond any husband and wife. Frustrating and discouraging days can feel as if trustworthy love is eroding. The key is to pursue this concise vision statement with honest communication, search for help in needed areas, and mutual forgiveness. The journey is for hearts of valor!

Reflective Questions on Trustworthy Love

Take time to reflect on your life realm of marriage or singleness as it relates to Trustworthy Love in your actions and attitudes.

1. If married, jot down some ways that you desire to grow in Trustworthy Love's actions and attitudes toward your husband.

   a. Doing good not harm toward your husband.

   b. Living out covenant love "all the days of her life" toward your husband.

2. If single, jot down some ways that you are living out your covenant love toward God and developing faithful and righteous relationships with others who call on God from a pure heart as stated in II Timothy 2:22.

2. HER HOME AND WORK

The portrait of our mentor of valor continues with clarity, as she lives and relates inside and outside her home. Inside her home, the fruit we will see is **Creative Diligence.** Outside her home, her fruit is **Profitable Enterprise.**

I provide a simple outline for the two fruits and her many actions and attitudes.

Inside Home (31:13-15)

Fruit--Creative Diligence

Actions	Attitudes
1. Picks material (13)	Eagerness (13)
2. Picks food (14)	Effortful (14)
3. Prepares food (15)	Discipline (15)

How does this wise woman spend a typical week? When we consider that a queen mother provides the specific strokes of form and color for her son, it is noteworthy that she composes actions and attitudes within a home and not a palace. Our mentor is a project manager who values the details of daily living. With creative diligence, she prepares for the many needs of her loved ones. On a questionnaire, she would state that one of her roles in life is a homemaker, as she diligently creates her home into what God wants it to be.

Some of us struggle to accept the title 'homemaker' as one of our callings in life. In reality, whether single or married, we all spend time each day preparing our food and clothing. Yes, it can often seem mundane and repetitive to fix one more meal and wash one more outfit.

In his book, **Dream Big, Think Small,** Pastor Jeff Manion builds upon what he observed from thirty consistent years of ministry. "A remarkable life is built by taking a thousand unremarkable steps. What if living a life of greatness for God is not about doing a few great things, but instead living a life of holy redundancy—showing up faithfully day after day in the seemingly little things? Stewardship! What if our greatest investments are faithfully raising our family, building a God-honoring career, cultivating a healthy heart, and developing strong friendships?"

Let's follow our guide into her home and watch her fruit of Creative Diligence displayed in three actions and attitudes.

1. Creative Diligence

Action--Picks materials for her family

She seeks wool and flax, (31:13a)

In her day, they used wool for clothing along with flax for linen thread. Today, we gather our wool and flax from T.J. Maxx, Zulily, Amazon, and other favorite stores. Industry and technology progressively remove much of our manual labor. Preparing the wardrobe for ourselves and family involves creative diligence as we pick the best places and prices to buy our clothes and material.

Attitude is Eagerness

and works with willing hands. (31:13b)

She not only labors diligently, but with a willingly delight as she takes on the responsibilities of her family. She finds pleasure in her work and considers that labor is good and idleness is unwise. With all our modern conveniences, we can minimize the value of enjoying the basic actions of life. Our mentor models that she intends to live her life's moments to the full. "So, whether you eat or drink, or whatever you do, do all to the glory of God" (1 Corinthians 10:31).

2. Creative Diligence

She is like the ships of the merchant;
she brings her food from afar. (31:14)

Action--Picks food for her family

Here the queen mother is painting the valorous woman like merchant ships. She is a visionary, who believes in giving extra effort as she chooses what is best for her family. She knows how to invest time and energy in places that will produce eternal dividends. Her search is diligent as she seeks creative ways to find healthy and economic resources to nourish her growing family.

Attitude is Effortful

Whether it is the local grocery store, farmers market, Amazon pantry, or her garden, our mentor leans into each task with an effortful spirit. Her focus is on her family, as she lovingly seeks to meet their needs.

---

3. Creative Diligence

She rises while it is yet night and provides food for her
household and portions for her maidens. (31:15)

Action--Prepares food for her family

These tasks may seem simple, but the practical care of a family and household are not always ingrained in us from our upbringing. The need to be reminded of the high value of caring for the basic needs of our family to be clothed and fed is part of this excellent woman's everyday life. If we are a natural at this, we are encouraged to continue.

"She rises while it is yet night." How many women today honestly rise before dawn on a regular basis? An essential household element for our mentor was the lamps that continually burned in the Jewish homes. The careful homemaker arose during the night to replenish the needed oil. Often she stayed up and started her household work of preparing for the first meal for her family and maidens(helpers). The fact that she had helpers for her work may not seem fair to many of us.

Often we are on our own as we try to meet our family's needs without resources for extra help. As the queen painting this portrait for her son, she revealed the value of a woman, who could oversee others to accomplish tasks. We have come a long way from the days of:

- Food preparation without a stove and microwave
- Making clothes without a Singer sewing machine or bargains at T.J. Maxx
- Cleaning the house without a Hoover vacuum and Mr. Clean

In today's world, we have these and many other electrical servants. I am very grateful for our modern conveniences!

Attitude is Discipline

A key lesson from the fifteenth verse is to see how this woman of valor disciplines her time to prepare for her busy days. A day planned and prayed over is a day with increased possibilities of smoothness and productivity. Her creative diligence with attitudes of eagerness, effort, and discipline toward her daily details reminds me of this Michelangelo story.

> Michelangelo was sculpting a figure from a block of marble with a friend observing him. The friend left and came back three months later and said, "I see that you haven't been working on your statue." Michelangelo answered, "Oh yes!" But to the observer, it seemed the same. The great artist replied, "Oh no, I have softened this line here, the hem of his garment. That might seem like a trifle, but it is in the trifles that bring perfection."

Our fruitful mentor is modeling that she values her family. She approaches the daily trifles of life as one shaping an incredible sculpture. As a woman of valor, she does not believe the details of her home are just problems to solve quickly. With focused attention, she allows **creative discipline** to launch her into a new day. Thankful for the gift of life and those in her care, she uniquely takes on each task with her splash of creativity. The colors that she paints her home wrap her husband, children, and those in her care with a sense of security, peace, and focused attention.

Walking Past My Sleeping Children by Ulrich Schaffer

It is early morning
and I have just walked past my sleeping children
Once again I am struck
By how great my responsibility is
How important my actions and being are
For the future of their lives

I can open the world to them
Convey the mystery of a beautiful plant
Or close them with an indoctrination of fear
I can help them toward being fully human
Or I can cripple them by narrow-mindedness
I can encourage them to reach out to others
Or turn around themselves egotistically
I can promote growth or stagnation

I can talk about respect
But not respect them
My words will be empty
And cause confusion
I can talk about openness
And be closed to their growing questions
My words will cause bewilderment

I can talk about discipline
But not practice self-discipline
In my eating, talking, reading, and watching TV
My words will be hollow
And cause turmoil

God I am Your child
And You are my perfect Father
Who teaches me responsibility, love, and care
And opens to me some of the mysteries of life
My great hope is that some of what I am learning from You
Will rub off and become visible as a father (mother) to my children.

Proverbs 31:16-19 provides a picture of our woman of valor and her accomplishments outside her home. After addressing her key priorities of her husband and household, she now has the time to pursue other skills and interests outside her home.

Outside Home (31:16-19)

Fruit--Profitable Enterprise

Actions | **Attitudes**

Actions
1. Profitable trading   (16)
2. Plants vineyard   (16)
3. Ponders effectiveness (18)
4. Prepares materials   (19)

Attitudes
Precise judgments   (16)
Passionate strength   (17)
Pleasurable satisfaction (18)
Persistent in tasks   (19)

1. Profitable Enterprise

She considers a field and buys it; (31:16a)

Action--Profitable Trading

Our biblical mentor knows how to network with her world. We saw how she picked out the material and food to meet her family's needs with creative diligence. Now she considers purchasing a particular field. Her action to buy land shows the strength of mind to encounter a challenging project.

Attitude is Precise Judgment

Our mentor embarks on enterprise ventures with research and dialogue. She knows that her skills can provide profit for her family. As a woman of valor, she is not fearful, but precise. She buys the field with the goal to plant a vineyard. Her decisiveness comes from consistently making wise decisions within her home and knowing what will bless her family.

---

2. Profitable Enterprise

with the fruit of her hands she plants a vineyard. (31:16b)

Action--Plants vineyard from earnings

Our woman of valor reinvests useful resources for her family. She connects with her culture through her business savvy. We might not expect the Bible to promote the business dealings outside the home of a wife and mother, especially with the highly patriarchal nature of the ancient world. However, in this inspired vision, the young king is encouraged to seek a woman who is comfortable in the competitive world outside her home. Her enterprising ambitions continue to show great stewardship of her abilities and relational skills in balance with her family priorities. The definition of enterprise is a venture that calls for courage and energy with a willingness to undertake bold projects.

Many of us may not be skilled at land investments or planting vineyards. The source of our actions outside the home comes from the gifts and abilities that God gives to us. The New Testament parable of the talents in Matthew 25 reminds us not to hide or waste our God-given resources. When we effectively use the resources He gives us, the Lord's response is "Well done, good and faithful servant! You have been faithful with a few things; I will put you in charge of many things. Come and share your master's happiness" (Matthew 25:21 NIV). His response is entirely different to the one who does not use the resources given to him, "You wicked, lazy servant! So you knew that I harvest where I have not sown and gather where I have not scattered seed? Well then, you should have put my money on deposit with the bankers, so that when I returned I would have received it back with interest" (Matthew 25: 26 NIV). We glorify God by our hard work in this world He created for us to cultivate.

Attitude is Passionate strength

17 She dresses herself with strength
and makes her arms strong. (31:17)

Repeatedly, we see why she is called a woman of valor. The fact that she dresses with strength and her arms are strong indicate wise choices and hard work. The future king is encouraged to seek a woman who wears strength in body, mind, and spirit. In Proverbs 1:1-9 his mother challenged the king to be a man of valor. "Do not give your strength to women, your ways to those who destroy kings" (Proverbs 1:3). She wants him to seek a wise woman with passionate strength, not the unwise woman of Proverbs 5:10,11, "who will take their fill of your strength and at the end of your life make you groan."

---

3. Profitable Enterprise

She sees that her trading is profitable,
and her lamp does not go out at night. (31:18)

Action--Ponders effectiveness

After her beneficial trading day, our mentor evaluates her efforts and activities. Back home in the quiet of the evening with a cup of decaf coffee, she enjoys some reflective time. As a good manager, she desires the right course for the efforts she initiates outside her home. Prayer before the Lord and interaction with her husband are part of her productive evaluation. If she finds negative results developing in the garden of her household, she recalibrates to keep her top priorities on her husband and family.

Attitude is Pleasurable Satisfaction

What flows out of this reflective time is the pleasurable satisfaction of goals set and work done with favorable outcomes. If we are too busy for this action of mindfulness, then we are too busy. Our next steps will tend to waver into waste and weariness. The pleasure and satisfaction from pondering the positives and negatives of the day provide fuel to spur her on to further effective action both inside and outside her home.

With her lamp on at night and children tucked into bed, we see our mentor comfortably engaged in the actions needed at the end of her day. With no TV available or printed book, her time at the spinning wheel is relaxing and profitable.

4. Profitable Enterprise

**She puts her hands to the distaff,
and her hands hold the spindle. (31:19)**

Action--Prepares Materials

We see her returning to finish the task of preparing materials as another part of her profitable enterprise, as well as the family provisions. Earlier in the day, she organized her time in verse 13 to have the fabric of wool and flax at home. Now she is ready to prepare materials for her family and home.

During 1,000 BC, she used the distaff, a type of spinning wheel. The distaff would hold the mass of flax material like a third hand. From it, she would spin the bulk material into the thread that would be used for clothes and other items needed in the home. Throughout history, women have dominated the field of sewing that takes much skill and patience.

Attitude is Persistence in tasks

Whether inside or outside of her home, our mentor knows that persistence is needed to turn creative diligence into profitable enterprise. Once again she dives into the details of a project to accomplish her goals. She keeps her priorities in mind and pursues her profits to minister to her Lord, husband, and family.

Reflective Questions on Her Home and Work

Take time to reflect on your Creative Diligence and Profitable Enterprise inside and outside your home from Proverbs 31:13-19. Focus on your attitudes and make them a praise and prayer list as you seek to grow in fruitfulness as a woman valor.

Inside Home
1. Creative Diligence

Actions	Attitudes
1. Picks material (13)	Eagerness (13)
2. Picks food (14)	Effortful (14)
3. Prepares food (15)	Discipline (15)

- Actions

- Attitudes

Outside Home
2. Profitable Enterprise

Actions	Attitudes
1. Profitable trading (16)	Precise judgments (16)
2. Plants vineyard (16)	Passionate strength (17)
3. Ponders effectiveness (18)	Pleasurable satisfaction (18)
4. Prepares materials (19)	Persistent in tasks (19)

- Actions

- Attitudes

Practical Planning ideas

- Take at least 10 minutes at the beginning of the day to plan and pray. Take another 10 minutes before going to bed to review your day and prepare for the next..

- What are your best methods to plan and review? Test out ways that will give you the 'pleasurable satisfaction' our mentor experienced.

  a. Make a note of your actions and to-dos along with your attitudes that need more growth.

  b. I have found a new Christian planner to be very effective It is called The Christian Planner and can be found online at christianplanner.com. It provides sections for goals, Christian growth disciplines, weekly and monthly schedule, quiet time notes, prayer requests, and general notes.

  c. Digital notebooks like Apple's Calendar, Notes and Evernote are great for keeping plans and reviews.

  d. Add your practical plans and ideas.

3. HER WORLD

Fruit of Loving Deeds

Actions	Attitudes
Provides for poor and needy (20)	Philanthropic giving (20)
Provides future for herself and family(21-22)	Peaceful, not fearful (21)
Provides respect for her husband (23)	Praise for husband (23)
Provides resources for family and world (23-24)	Proactively combines(24) skill with needs of world

1. Loving Deeds

She opens her hand to the poor
and reaches out her hands to the needy. (31:20)

Action--Provides for the poor and needy

The act of opening her hand in Hebrew means "with its nerves and sinews ready for exertion." We see this godly woman's genuine concern for those outside her family. She reaches out to the poor and needy in her world with her open hands and heart.

Attitude is Philanthropic Giving

Her attitude is philanthropic (generous, benevolent) giving. Proverbs 22:9 states, "A generous person will themselves be blessed for they share their food with the poor." John Leax's poem captures a glimpse of the valor of her loving deeds.

At The Winter Feed

His feather flame doused dull
by the icy cold,
The cardinal hunched
into the rough, green feeder,
but ate not seed.

Through binoculars
I saw festered and
useless his beak,
broken at the root.

Then two:
one blazing, one gray
rode the swirling
weather into my vision
and lighted at his side.

Unhurried,
as if possessing
the patience of God,
they cracked
sunflower seeds

and fed him beak to wounded beak choice meats.

Each morning and afternoon
the winter long
that old trio...that trinity of need,
returned and ate...their sacrament of broken seed.

As we ponder God's work through our mentor's actions and attitudes, let us surrender our hands to be used to touch and feed the needy of this world by **Loving Deeds.** The giving to the world with such compassion is an outflow of her focused priorities. Her firm foundation provides the needed balance to minister to the world.

In verses 21-24, we see a woman of valor and strength moving in and out of her home and world weaving the tapestry of her God-directed life.

2. Loving Deeds

She is not afraid of snow for her household,
for all her household are clothed in scarlet.
She makes bed coverings for herself;
her clothing is fine linen and purple. (31:21,22)

Action--Provides resources for their future

Our mentor's loving deeds of preparing and organizing her family's clothes before each season covers all of them with peace and preparation. She also carves out the time to make beautiful clothing and bed coverings. Her husband will appreciate such provisions. Purple and scarlet were colors used for quality clothes and other material in her day.

Attitude is Peaceful, not Fearful

Whether she is in or out of the home, she has a peaceful spirit, without the need to fear because she prepares and organizes for the future. Her Creative Discipline reduces stress and allows for Loving Deeds. Our mentor is known for her positive attitudes that bring peace, instead of fear and anxiety to those in her care.

3. Loving Deeds

**Her husband is known in the gates
when he sits among the elders of the land. (31:23)**

Action--Provides respect for husband

Maybe you have wondered where this blessed husband has been while his wife bears such abundant fruit! He is busy fulfilling his God-given responsibilities too. Her husband works at the city gate where he takes his seat with the other leaders of the land. 'In the gates' refers to governmental oversight. Remember this is a queen mother speaking about her son's role as the future king.

Attitude is Praise for husband

One of the keys to his prestige and position goes back to their marriage. The future woman of valor will bring him good, and not harm. "An excellent wife is the crown of her husband, but she who brings shame is like rottenness in his bones" (Proverbs 12:4). Her actions and attitudes bear the fruit of Proverbs 14:1, "The wisest of women builds her house, but folly with her own hands tears it down."

---

4. Loving Deeds

**She makes linen garments and sells them;
she delivers sashes to the merchant. (31:24)**

Action--Provides resources for family and world

In her world, our mentor impacts many people, because of her skillful artistry, sales, and profit in the marketplace. Her actions honor and profit her husband, family and herself as she deals with others.

Attitude is Proactive to combine her skills with needs of others

The details of clothes and decorating of the home have a place in a woman's life. We are to enjoy using our skills with a peaceful heart as we bless others. So far our journey with our mentor of valor encompasses her life realms of marriage, home, and work, as well as her world. Her fruit factor abundantly displays her **Creative Diligence, Profitable Enterprise, and Loving Deeds**.

Reflective Questions on Loving Deeds

Now take time to reflect on your fruitful actions of Loving Deeds.

How is the fruit of Loving Deeds growing in your life and world?

1. In Actions

2. In Attitudes

The Message

By Derick Gentry Thompson
from the album, *Rock Gospel of Jesus Christ*

Some things in life get so complex
You can't understand them
But how you live your life
Doesn't have to be that way

Maybe it seems natural or foreign
But your heart knows what's true

Cause it's so simple
Simply about love
Loving God and your neighbor

If you follow Christ, His life, His loves
It will be evident
To a world that's so lost in sin

The life that loves others first
Then serves itself
Cannot be hidden

Cause it's so simple
Simply about love
Loving God and your neighbor
Can you love when you are not loved back?

I am the way,
I am the truth,
I am the life.

Cause it's so simple
Simply about love
Loving God and your neighbor

Can you love when you are not loved back?
Love knows no greater
Than to lay down itself.

33

4. HER CHARACTER

In Her Spirit

Fruit of Strength and Dignity

Strength and dignity are her clothing,
and she laughs at the time to come. (31:25)

The Woman of Valor is known for her beautiful spirit that glows with strength and dignity. Those around her observe that she draws from an inner reservoir that fills her with such a joyful attitude toward the future.

Her clothing of strength and dignity provides:

With Strength
- Ability to endure
- Boldness and determination
- Courage as she faces challenges fearlessly

With Dignity
- Distinguished by deed and action
- Excellence in character
- Full of moral force and commitment to what is right

With such character bearing fruit, she does not have an attitude of fear, but joy and peace concerning the future, because her trust is in God.

Psalm 112:7 says, "He is not afraid of bad news; his heart is firm, trusting in the Lord." Her security in God's loving sovereignty is so steady that she can laugh out loud with joy assured of God's provision.

Story of a Woman of Valor with a spirit of Strength and Dignity

from the book, *Through Gates of Splendor* by Elisabeth Elliot

As a young missionary, Elisabeth Elliot traveled to Ecuador where she married fellow missionary, Jim Elliot. Sensing the call to share the gospel with an unreached people group, Jim, Elizabeth and four other missionary couples made contact with the Aucas, a tribe living in the Ecuadorian jungles.

With strength and dignity, Elizabeth and the other wives were able to smile at their future because they were grounded in God and His call. As the dangerous time neared for their missionary husbands to make contact with the Auca Indians she wrote,

"The other wives and I talked together one night about the possibility of becoming widows. What would we do? God gave us peace of heart, and confidence that whatever might happen, His Word would hold. We knew that 'when He puts forth His sheep, He goes before them.' God's leading was unmistakable up to this point. Each of us knew when we married our husbands that there would never be any question about who came first -- God and His work held first place in each life. It was the condition of true discipleship; it became devastatingly meaningful now."

Due to a tragic misunderstanding after much time trying to reach the Aucas, all five of the men were speared to death in a final encounter. After the death of their husbands, Elizabeth wrote, "The prayers of the widows themselves are for the Aucas. We look forward to the day when these savages will join us in Christian praise. Revenge? The thought never crossed the mind of one of the wives or other missionaries. God is God. If He is God, He is worthy of my worship and my service. I will find rest nowhere but in His will, and that will is infinitely, immeasurably, unspeakably beyond my largest notions of what He is up to. God is the God of human history, and He is at work continuously, mysteriously, accomplishing His eternal purposes in us, through us, for us, and in spite of us."

In Her Mouth

Fruit of Wisdom & Kindness

She opens her mouth with wisdom,
and the teaching of kindness is on her tongue. (31:26)

The woman of valor carries her spirit's strength and dignity into the realm of her speech. She removes herself from idle talk, gossip or slander with her mouth providing sentences of wisdom and kindness. She internalizes God's knowledge of His Word and imparts it to others. Alexander Maclaren, a Scottish theologian and author from the 19th century, described this kind of person as "one who seeks to cultivate a buoyant, joyous sense of the 'crowded kindnesses of God' in their daily life." Our mentor looks for opportunities to share God's kindnesses.

The Power of Words

A careless word may kindle strife

A cruel word may wreck a life

A bitter word may hate instill

A brutal word may smite and kill

A gracious word may smooth the way

A joyous word may light the day

A timely word may lessen stress

A loving word may heal and bless.

(from Paul Lee Tan, Encyclopedia of 7700 Illustrations)

In Her Eyes

Fruit of Spiritual Discernment

She looks well to the ways of her household
and does not eat the bread of idleness. (31:27)

A woman of valor cares about the actions and attitudes of herself, as well as her family. She lives, works, and plays with eyes of spiritual discernment. Her prayer and input into their lives keep watch with a vision to encourage good and restrain evil.

In this realm of spiritual, emotional, physical, and mental training, she knows the immense impact that her attitudes, actions, and words have on her children. She is busy with many responsibilities, but when it comes to her spiritual training of her children, they are her top priority.

5. HER REWARD

Fruit of Praise from family

Her children rise up and call her blessed; her husband also,
and he praises her: "Many women have done excellently,
but you surpass them all." (31:28,29)

When a woman receives praises and blessings from her children and husband, it is clear to others that the fruit of this woman's life is homegrown. Those who know us best will always feel the strongest about our strengths and weaknesses. In receiving such praise, she is offered appreciation, recognition, and a validation of her life as she lives and gives before her God and others.

What are the praises given to this Woman of Valor, their mother, and wife? It is the abundant fruit of her life:

- Trustworthy Love
- Creative Diligence
- Profitable Enterprise
- Loving Deeds
- Character in Spirit of Strength and Dignity, in her Mouth with Wisdom and Kindness and her Eyes with Spiritual Discernment

If the summary of her actions and attitudes were the central message this inspired mother desired to give her son, it would be a challenge for any woman to meet up to such high standards. In verse 31:30, the prayerful mother draws his attention and ours to the secret source that provides the true strength and power for the woman of valor.

Her Secret Source

Rooted in the Fear of God

**Charm is deceitful, and beauty is vain,
but a woman who fears the Lord is to be praised. (31:30)**

A charming personality or beautiful woman is not to be the future king's quest,
but a woman praised because of her eternal source of fruitfulness.
The Proverbs 31 woman is "**a woman who fears the Lord.**"

When I arrived at this verse in my study years ago, I was challenged to dig into a deeper understanding of what it meant to 'fear the Lord'. All the other verses talk about the fruitfulness of a wise woman's life. This verse describes her relationship with her Lord and the root system growing in this amazing woman! That will be our focus in the next section.

In summary, after all the busyness, interaction, and character of our woman of valor, we see in this verse the quiet chamber of her inner strength and success of her life. The life she lives is one rooted in the study of the Word of God and worship of Him as the top priority. She knows that the happiness of her marriage, home, and life depends on the favor of her Heavenly Father above all people, actions, and possessions.

The final verse of Proverbs 31 jubilantly states:

Give her of the fruit of her hands, and let her works praise her in the gates. (31:31)

Her noble character, godly actions, and attitudes will bring her honor and recognition from leaders of the nation. Her life is a tree full of fruit, not withering leaves. The young king is to seek a woman who recognizes the impact of her actions and attitudes and holds herself accountable for her choices before God.

We might inwardly wonder—Does she have any problems? Is anyone that perfect? The verses have no hint of failure. Let's not forget; this Proverb is prayerful and inspired poetry. The beautiful vision paints the portrait of wisdom lived through a woman's life. The Lord knows we need our vision renewed in this challenging world.

We discovered her strong Fruit Factor has the secret source of a 'fear of God' heart. The following song by Ken Medema describes the fruit, root and soil factors of the Rooted Woman of Valor.

The Tree Song

By Ken Medema

I saw a tree by the riverside one day as I walked along,
Straight as an arrow pointing to the sky growing tall and strong.
How do you grow so tall and strong I said to the riverside tree?
This is the song that my tree friend sang to me:

(Chorus)
I've got roots growing down to the water,
I've got leaves growing up to the sunshine,
And the fruit is a sign of the life in me.
I am shade from the hot summer sundown,
I am nest for the birds of the heaven.
I'm becoming what the Lord of trees has meant me to be.

I saw a tree in the wintertime when snow lay on the ground,
Straight as an arrow and pointing to the sky
and winter winds blew all around,
How do you stay so tall and strong I said to the wintertime tree?
This is the song that my tree friend sang to me:
(Chorus above)

I saw a tree in the city streets where buildings blocked the sun,
Green and lovely I could see it gave joy to everyone.
How do you grow in the city streets I said to the downtown tree?
This is the song that my tree friend sang to me:
(Chorus above)

Reflective Questions on the Woman of Valor

As you pray to become the tall and strong tree the Lord meant you to be, review each fruit of the Proverbs 31 woman of valor. Jot down a specific way that you are growing in each fruit. Then, jot down a specific way you know you need to grow in each area of fruitfulness.

1. Her Marriage/Relationships
Fruit-Trustworthy Love

2. Her Home & Work

Inside Home
Fruit-Creative Diligence
with attitudes of Eagerness, Effort, Discipline

Outside Home
Fruit-Profitable Enterprise
with attitudes of Precision, Passion, Pleasurable Satisfaction and Persistence

3. Her World
Fruit-Loving Deeds
with Philanthropic Giving, Peaceful, Praise for husband, and Proactively combining her skills with needs of others

4. Her Character

    Fruit-Strength and Dignity in her spirit

    Fruit-Wisdom & Kindness in her mouth

    Fruit-Spiritual Discernment in her eyes

5. Her Rewards
    Fruit-Praised by family and others

2. Draw a tree that reflects the fruit of your life
like the Proverbs 31 woman of valor on page 40.
(For example, strong fruit in marriage, withered fruit in world,
budding fruit in family)

3. What weeds are hampering your growth? Be honest!

Small Group Interaction

1. Share in your small group some of your reflections.

2. Share one key area that you want your group to pray for concerning your growth in fruitfulness.

3. Pray together for each other by praying for the person on your right.

Proverbs 31:10-31 English Acrostic

Jan C Thompson's English version adapted from ESV

10 **A woman of valor** who can find? She is far more precious than jewels.

11 **Benevolent** heart of her husband trusts in her, and he will have no lack of gain.

12 She **Chooses for** him good, and not harm, all the days of her life.

13 She **Diligently** seeks wool and flax, and works with willing hands.

14 She **Exemplifies** the ships of the merchant; she brings her food from afar.

15 She **First** rises while it is yet night and provides food for her household and portions for her maidens.

16 She **Gives thought** to a field and buys it; with the fruit of her hands she plants a vineyard.

17 She **Habitually** dresses herself with strength and makes her arms strong.

18 She **Identifies** that her merchandise is profitable. Her lamp does not go out at night.

19 She **Joins** her hands to the distaff, and her hands hold the spindle.

20 She **Kindly** opens her hand to the poor and reaches out her hands to the needy.

21 She **Lives** not afraid of snow for her household, for all her household are clothed in scarlet.

22 She **Makes** bed coverings for herself; her clothing is fine linen and purple.

23 Her **Notable** husband is known in the gates when he sits among the elders of the land.

24 She **Originates** linen garments and sells them; she delivers sashes to the merchant.

25 **Power** and dignity are her clothing, and she laughs at the time to come.

26 She **Quietly** opens her mouth with wisdom, and the teaching of kindness is on her tongue.

27 She **Reviews** well to the ways of her household and does not eat the bread of idleness.

28 Her children **Stand up** and call her blessed; her husband also, and he praises her:

29 "**Thousands of women** have done excellently, but you surpass them all."

30 **Ungodly Charm** is deceitful, and beauty is vain, but **a woman who fears the Lord is to be praised.**

31 **Vouchsafe** the fruit of her hands, and let her works praise her in the gates.

- **Watch** her with amazement!
- **eXamine** her to find how to be a Rooted Woman of Valor.
- **Zero** in on this woman of valor as your mentor and your friend.

An **acrostic** is a poem (or another form of writing) in which the first letter (or syllable, or word) of each line (or paragraph, or other recurring feature in the text) spells out a word, message or the alphabet. The word comes from the French *acrostiche* from post-classical Latin *acrostichis*, from Koine Greek ἀκροστιχίς, from Ancient Greek ἄκρος "highest, topmost" and στίχος "verse"). As a form of constrained writing, an acrostic can be used as a mnemonic device to aid memory retrieval.

Root Factor

of the

Woman of Valor

Root Factor of the Woman of Valor

The portrait of our Proverbs 31 mentor revealed her leafy branches bearing fruit in abundance. We tasted the various fruit of her life in the realms of her marriage, home, work, world, and character. Her rewards challenged us to grow in fruitfulness as we observed her actions and attitudes. Proverbs 31:30 reveals the source of the strength and rootedness of the woman of valor.

Charm is deceitful, and beauty is vain,
but a woman who fears the Lord is to be praised. (31:30)

The king's mother wisely led the focus of her son's search to a woman who had a 'fear of God' heart. When he found a woman who bore the fruit and attitudes of the Proverbs 31 vision, he was to see if her heart was rooted in the 'fear of God', not charm or outside beauty.

Now it is time to look below the fruitfulness of our woman of valor to the roots that nourish her praiseworthy life. In reality, the topic of roots was never on my 'to write' list. I am not a gardener, nor do I come from a family tree of anything more than a few patriarchal tomato plants. My hyper-aversion to bugs is well-known to my family, who come running at my knee-jerk screams. "How can a tiny bug produce such a reaction in you, Mom?"

Rooted Journey

The idea of giving more thought to the underground life and roots of this woman of valor slowly sprouted during my in-depth study of her fruitful actions and attitudes. I wrote in my journal at the beginning of that year.

A new year,

some tears, some cheer,

Thoughts wander to future days,

Now all appears in a haze

A puzzle with pieces cut out by God

Shaped and fitted into our life's sod.

The roots of a tree serve to anchor it to the ground while they gather water and nutrients for all its parts. Roots provide defense, survival, energy storage, and many other resources. In this chapter, our goal is to understand the 'fear of God' root factor of our Proverbs 31 woman of valor. By digging into this biblical concept, we can bring to light the depth of her root system that only God creates.

"All that is gold does not glitter,

Not all those who wander are lost;

The old that is strong does not wither,

Deep roots are not reached by the frost."

— J.R.R. Tolkien, 'The Fellowship of the Ring"

Key Factors of the Rooted Woman of Valor

1. Benefits of the Fear of God

First, we will dig into the rich earth of Scripture to root out the many benefits for those who understand and live in the true 'fear of God.' We will discover how each area of the woman of valor's life realms are nourished and supported by her 'fear of God' root system.

2. Heart of the Fear of God

Next, we will discover the heart of the 'fear of God.' We will look at the Biblical definition and clear stages that must be journeyed to have a heart that understands the 'fear of God.' We will meet a key Biblical example, who is known as one who feared God.

3. Growing Fear of God Roots

Finally, we will dig through selected Scripture seeking to understand how to develop a strong root system that will sustain a fruitful 'fear of God' heart as a woman of valor.

1. Benefits of the Fear of God

Benefits are a great motivation when we are challenged to grow in specific areas of our lives. The Bible provides a treasure chest of benefits for those who 'fear God'. Our Proverbs 31 mentor is a perpetual beneficiary, as one whose heart roots have grown deep in the 'fear of God.' Let's look at her five life realms to discover God's encouragement to nurture our faith and desire to be a woman who understands the 'fear of God'. We will consider two benefit verses for each area. At the end of this section, I provide a list of more benefit verses.

Her Marriage--Trustworthy Love

Developing a trustworthy love toward our husband over a lifetime will have its challenges. Issues will emerge that have the potential to weaken our mutual trust. If we are leaning on our strength and wisdom to have a good marriage, we will find our resources limited. We need a deep-seated source of love and trust that comes from 'fearing God.' He offers us His steadfast love, His attention, and listening ear to provide His river of resources to love others.

The Lord takes pleasure in **those who fear him,** in those who hope in his steadfast love. (Psalm 147:11)

Then **those who feared the Lord** spoke with one another. The Lord paid attention and heard them, and a book of remembrance was written before him of those who **feared the Lord** and esteemed his name. (Malachi 3:16)

When a woman receives such nourishment to her soul from the Lord, she grows roots that draw from a God-given source with a depth of love and maturity toward her husband and others.

Her Home--Creative Diligence

When it comes to the details of work inside her home, the benefits of being a woman who 'fears God', provide needed support. She knows as she gets up early to pick out materials and food for the needs of her family, God is always her refuge and shelter. Instead of being lonely as she pushes through the details of the day, she communes with her God. She knows that her strong confidence and courage are of God, not herself, to provide a sheltering home for her children and husband.

Oh, how abundant is your goodness, which you have stored up for **those who fear You** and worked for those who take refuge in you, in the sight of the children of mankind! (Psalm 31:19)

In the **fear of the Lord** one has strong confidence, and his children will have a refuge. (Proverbs 14:26)

A beautiful example of bearing fruit in the everyday details of life comes from the book, *Practicing the Presence of God.* Brother Lawrence's role in the monastery was to take care of kitchen details. He shared the secret to his heart's perspective on daily work. "We ought not to be weary of doing little things for the love of God, who regards not the greatness of the work, but the love with which it is performed."

Her Work--Profitable Enterprise

As our woman of valor moves outside her home to accomplish profitable enterprise to benefit family and herself, she continues to be aware of the Lord's presence and provision. Her goals and plans seek to keep God's values in mind. His wisdom has taught her that His blessing is a great treasure, even if it seems small to the world.

> Blessed is **everyone who fears the Lord**, who walks in his ways!
> You shall eat the fruit of the labor of your hands; you shall be
> blessed, and it shall be well with you. (Psalm 128:1,2)

> Better is a little with the **fear of the Lord** than great treasure
> and trouble with it. (Proverbs 15:16)

Her World--Loving Deeds

Along with the priorities of her husband and family at home and work, she takes the time to reach out to the poor and needy. Her actions and attitudes are rooted in the compassion that she receives from her Heavenly Father. As she shares this empathy with the world, she accompanies it with the message of God's salvation, wisdom, knowledge, and glory.

> As a father shows compassion to his children,
> so the Lord shows compassion to **those who fear him**.
> (Psalm 103:13)

> Surely his salvation is near to **those who fear him**,
> that glory may dwell in our land. (Psalm 85:9)

> And He will be the stability of your times, abundance of
> salvation, wisdom, and knowledge; **the fear of the Lord**
> is Zion's treasure. (Isaiah 33:6)

Her Character

Her character is rooted in the integrity of the God she worships. As He mentors her through His Word and Spirit, her strength, dignity, wisdom, kindness, and discernment find their source in following His ways.

Strength and Dignity in her Spirit

By steadfast love and faithfulness iniquity is atoned for, and by **the fear of the Lord** one turns away from evil. (Proverbs 16:6)

Wisdom and Kindness in her Mouth

The **fear of the Lord** is the beginning of knowledge; (Proverbs 1:7)
The **fear of the Lord** is the beginning of wisdom,
and the knowledge of the Holy One is insight. (Proverbs 9:10)

Spiritual Discernment in her Eyes

Behold, the eye of the Lord is on **those who fear Him**, on those who hope in His steadfast love, that He may deliver their soul from death and keep them alive in famine. (Psalms 33:18,19)

Her Reward--Praise of family

The reward for humility and **fear of the Lord** is riches and honor and life. (Proverbs 22:4)

Blessed is everyone who **fears the Lord**, who walks in his ways! You shall eat the fruit of the labor of your hands; you shall be blessed, and it shall be well with you. Your wife will be like a fruitful vine within your house; your children will be like olive shoots around your table. (Psalm 128:1-3)

The abundance of Scriptures on the benefits of a heart that 'fears God' can continually motivate us to desire the root system of our Proverbs 31 mentor. The verses on the following page offer more benefits for the heart that fears God.

Fear of God Benefits Verses

Look up some of these 'fear of God' benefit verses and spend time praising God for his generous benefits and blessings.

1. Isaiah 33:6
2. Job 28:28
3. Psalm 31:19
4. Psalm 34:7
5. Psalm 34:9
6. Psalm 34:11-12
7. Psalm 85:9
8. Psalm 25:14
9. Psalm 33:18,19
10. Psalm 103:11
11. Psalm 103:13
12. Psalm 147:11
13. Malachi 3:16,17
14. Psalm 128
15. Proverbs 1:7
16. Proverbs 9:10
17. Proverbs 10:27
18. Proverbs 14:26
19. Proverbs 14:27
20. Proverbs 15:16
21. Proverbs 16:6
22. Proverbs 19:23
23. Proverbs 22:4

2. Heart of the Fear of God

With the bounty of benefits for the 'fear of God' heart, we are greatly encouraged to become this wise and highly praised woman. My question in my early study of Proverbs 31 was, "I want to be this fruitful and wise woman, but what is a practical definition of a 'fear of God' heart?" The Lord promises to provide not only benefits but clarification for what He asks of us on our spiritual journey. Sometimes we feel like we still don't understand.

On my spiritual journey when I don't understand God's truth, it is often because:

- I have never been taught or searched the Scriptures myself about a specific issue like the 'fear of God.'
- I am ignoring the truths I already know because my heart is pursuing its direction.

As a young mom, I had not studied the 'fear of God', nor had I received clear teaching or practical understanding of it. As we dig into its meaning and application, I pray you will find that clear understanding and new confidence of being rooted as a 'fear of God' woman.

Definition of the Fear of God

Two key passages that define what it means to 'fear God':

> **The fear of the Lord** is to **hate evil;** Pride and arrogance and
> the way of evil and perverted speech I hate. (Proverbs 8:13)

> Come, O children, listen to me; **I will teach you the fear of the
> Lord.** What man is there who desires life and loves many days,
> that he may see good?   Keep your tongue from evil and your lips
> from speaking deceit. **Turn away from evil** and do good; seek
> peace and pursue it. (Psalm 34:11-14)

Basic Definition--To fear God is to hate evil and turn away from it.

Five stages in Scripture must be understood and processed for us to become
deeply rooted in the 'fear of God.'

Five Stages of understanding the Fear of God

Stage 1 No fear of God

There is **no fear of God** before their eyes. (Romans 3:18)

Romans 1:21-31 explains that God reveals Himself to humankind through
creation. Men and women have turned from God since their fall in the Garden
of Eden toward evil, including idolatry, sinful desires, depraved minds and
more. Even though they knew God, they did not honor Him as God.

Definition of Evil

> Though they know God's righteous decree that those who
> practice such things deserve to die, they not only do them
> but give approval to those who practice them. (Romans 1:32)

> Transgression speaks to the wicked deep in his heart; there is
> **no fear of God before his eyes.** For he flatters himself in his
> own eyes that his iniquity cannot be found out and hated. He
> plots trouble while on his bed; he sets himself in a way that is
> not good; **he does not reject evil**. (Psalm 36:1b,2,4)

Stage 2 Fear of Punishment

We see Stage 2 in the vivid portrait of Adam and Eve in Genesis 3. God created man and woman without sin. Initially, humankind had a close relationship with their Creator. Then, Eve decided after her conversation with the serpent to ignore God's Word and believe the serpent's misguided directions.

> "Did God actually say, 'You shall not eat of the tree in the garden'?"
> The serpent said to the woman, "You will not surely die."
> (Genesis 3:1b,4)

The disregard for God's wisdom led to the severing of Adam and Eve's close relationship with their Creator. Immediately, they were aware of their sin by recognizing their nakedness and need for a covering. When God came to meet them, they sensed the guilt from turning toward evil and the fear of punishment that God promised.

> And they heard the sound of the Lord God walking in the garden
> in the cool of the day, and the man and his wife hid themselves
> from the presence of the Lord God among the trees of the garden.
>
> But the Lord God called to the man and said to him, "Where
> are you?" And he said, "I heard the sound of you in the garden,
> and I was afraid, because I was naked, and I hid myself."
>
> He said, "Who told you that you were naked? Have you eaten of
> the tree of which I commanded you not to eat?" (Genesis 3:8-10)

The fear of punishment appeared in the Garden of Eden, as God warned. The serpent embodied Stage 1 'No Fear of God' and led Adam and Eve through the door of Stage 2 'Fear of Punishment,' where he tempted them to follow.

A Situation

Lyrics by Derick Gentry Thompson
From Strive's album, *The Story Before*
'God's thoughts after the Fall'

This is going to be tough

Because we have a situation

That requires a new look.

Look, Look, Look

We're going to look there

You made a choice

Just when you think you know something

You know nothing

Brace yourself now for what is coming.

Got a couple of questions

and they are going to demand an answer.

No more lying, let's have the truth now

So you feel so guilty?

Going round and round and round.

Don't try to fool Me now

Here is what I say...

Everything, everything you wanted

Is this how you thought it would end?

Down the road, down the road so unsupported

But then you are just human.

Stage 2 Fear of Punishment (Continued)

God sets boundaries for humans, but they do not obey Him. Since the Fall, all humans enter the world in Stage 1. As stated in Romans 3:23, "For all have sinned and fall short of the glory of God." To fear punishment is not to fear God and hate sin, as clarified in Proverbs 8:13. Instead of hating sin, man's greatest regret is that God hates sin. If convinced that God, as Judge, would regard sin lightly, humans' shallow fear of Him would collapse.

This dilemma developed in the Garden of Eden—God hates evil—man loves it. All false religions spark from this collision. Man tries to appease God's anger over his sin. Though he feels a need for a clear conscience and freedom from guilt, he is often unwilling to take God's path and turn from the evil. So he tends to invent other ways to gain peace.

> And they sewed fig leaves together and made themselves
> loincloths. And they heard the sound of the Lord God walking
> in the garden in the cool of the day, and the man and his wife hid
> from the presence of the Lord God. (Genesis 3:7b,8)

> They exchanged the truth about God for a lie and worshiped and
> served the creature rather than the Creator. (Romans 1:25)

Because the "wages or penalty for sin is death" as Romans 3:23 states, only when God covers us with His remedy for sin will we be forgiven and find His peace. "And the Lord God made for Adam and his wife garments of skins and clothed them." (Genesis 3:21)

This first animal sacrifice for sin came with the promise of the Messiah as the only perfect sacrifice. "He (Christ) shall bruise your (the serpent's) head, and you (the serpent) will bruise His heel." (Genesis 3:15b)

Later, God directed His people through Moses to regularly sacrifice animals as a reminder of His promised provision for sin's covering. "The law is only a shadow of the good things that are coming—not the realities themselves. For this reason, it can never, by the same sacrifices repeated endlessly year after year, make perfect those who draw near to worship." (Hebrews 10:1 NIV)

The Overture

Lyrics by Derick Gentry Thompson

from Strive album, **Rock Gospel of Jesus Christ**

What is this that man has done

Broken all My sacred trust

And let sin destroy all your beauty

And now there is only one way to restore

You to Me...

To Me...

My Son, your Savior

Stage 3 Facing Sin and God's Sacrifice

We must accept God's sacrifice, instead of trying to produce personal sacrifices to appease Him.

> But now apart from the law the righteousness of God has been made known, to which the Law and the Prophets testify. This righteousness is given through faith in Jesus Christ to all who believe. There is no difference between Jew and Gentile, for all have sinned and fall short of the glory of God, and all are justified freely by his grace through the redemption that came by Christ Jesus. God presented Christ as a sacrifice of atonement, through the shedding of his blood—to be received by faith. He did this to demonstrate his righteousness, because in his forbearance he had left the sins committed beforehand unpunished. (Romans 3:21-25 NIV)

God presented Christ as the sacrifice of atonement through faith in His shed blood for us on the cross. We must accept God's only way for sin and evil to be forgiven. Christ forgives our sin by trusting Him. At that point, we begin to hate sin instead of just fearing punishment.

> For he himself is our peace, who has made the two groups one and has destroyed the barrier, the dividing wall of hostility, by setting aside in his flesh the law with its commands and regulations. His purpose was to create in himself one new humanity out of the two, thus making peace, and in one body to reconcile both of them to God through the cross, by which he put to death their hostility. He came and preached peace to you who were far away and peace to those who were near. For through him we both have access to the Father by one Spirit. (Ephesians 2:14-18 NIV)

We can be reconciled with God when we agree that Jesus is our peace, who has taken our sin away by His one sacrifice.

Stage 4 Forgiven and Hates Sin

Instead of hating God for His holiness, the forgiven person instinctively hates the evil of his own heart and longs for the day when all things shall be made new by their Lord and Creator.

> However, to the one who does not work but trusts God who justifies the ungodly, their faith is credited as righteousness. David says the same thing when he speaks of the blessedness of the one to whom God credits righteousness apart from works: "Blessed are those whose transgressions are forgiven, whose sins are covered. Blessed is the one whose sin the Lord will never count against them." (Romans 4:5-8 NIV)

A person moves from Stage 3 'Facing Sin and God's Sacrifice' to Stage 4 'Forgiven and Hates Sin,' when they acknowledge the sacrificial death and resurrection of Jesus Christ for their sins. **Only at that point, do we begin to truly understand what it means to have a 'fear of God' heart like the Proverbs 31 woman.**

The entering into a clear understanding of the 'fear of God' is like the seed of a tree. It is the spiritual beginning and birth of a person with the potential of the fruitful life God intends for each of us. God said in Romans 8:15, "The Spirit you received does not make you slaves, so that you live in fear again; rather, the Spirit you received brought your adoption to sonship. And by him we cry, "Abba, Father." (NIV)

When we by faith receive God's covering for our sin, we no longer need to fear God's wrath and punishment. In a sense, the sin encasement of our life's seed opens. We begin to grow spiritually and know the God who loves us. If before today you have not faced your sin and received forgiveness by journeying through 'Fear of God' Stages 1-4 explained from the Scriptures, you can do that by prayer. Pray to the Lord admitting your sin and ask for God's forgiveness through the sacrifice of His Son, Jesus Christ. When we come to realize that we hate sin like God does and need to trust His way for forgiveness, the eternal cleansing and birth into His family take place.

"With His own pierced hands, Jesus created a pasture for the soul.
He tore out the thorny underbrush of condemnation.
He pried loose the huge boulders of sin.
In their place He planted seeds of grace and dug ponds of mercy.
And He invites us to rest there."
(from the book, *Traveling Light,* by Max Lucado)

Stage 5 Maturing Fear of God Heart

This precious heart of the 'fear of God' woman provides the source of the valor we see in her life. She is forgiven of her sin and now free to grow in an understanding of God and the fruitful life He wants to bring forth in her. The following acrostic on FEAR is the summary I gleaned from the Scriptures on the definition of the fear of God. By understanding these key factors, I began to have a clear and practical application of one who 'fears God.'

- **Forsake** (to reject and leave behind)
  Evil (what God calls sin and disobedience to Him in our actions and attitudes)

- **Acknowledge** God in every part of my life, instead of going my way.
  "Trust in the Lord with all your heart, and do not lean on your own understanding. In all your ways **acknowledge him**, and he will make straight your paths. Be not wise in your own eyes; **fear the Lord,** and turn away from evil. It will be healing to your flesh and refreshment to your bones." (Proverbs 3:5-8)

- **Reverence** and worship of our Holy God. This is respect mixed with love and awe of the One we desire to obey. We have a desire to give our heart and lives to glorify Him, not ourselves.
  "Therefore, I urge you, brothers and sisters, in view of God's mercy, to offer your bodies as a living sacrifice, holy and pleasing to God—this is **your true and proper worship**. Do not conform to the pattern of this world, but be transformed by the renewing of your mind. Then you will be able to test and approve what God's will is—his good, pleasing and perfect will." (Romans 12:1,2 NIV)

This acrostic provides a practical definition of the 'fear of God.' Our heart roots grow as we obey God's Word and turn from sin and evil that displeases Him. We acknowledge and reverence Him as the Gardener of our soul. As Pat Palau says in her book, **Scared to Death**, "My fear shows what, or who, I trust."

Just as a child does not naturally fear fire, we must learn to recognize the 'fear of God' with its remarkable potential for benefit and destruction. We must learn to forsake evil, acknowledge and reverence our Lord in every area of our life. God tells us to fear Him and acknowledge His character of justice, holiness, omniscience and all He is in His Word. In the Bible, God gives us a clear example of a man, who is known to live out the 'fear of God.' Let's dig into his life and see how his 'fear of God' heart roots grow.

.

Biblical Example of the Fear of God

Backstory from Job 1

One day the angels came to present themselves before the Lord, and Satan also came with them. The Lord said to Satan, "Where have you come from?" Satan answered the Lord, "From roaming throughout the earth, going back and forth on it." Then the Lord said to Satan, "Have you considered **my servant Job?** There is no one on earth like him; he is blameless and upright,

a man who fears God and shuns evil.

"Does Job fear God for nothing?" Satan replied. "Have you not put a hedge around him and his household and everything he has? You have blessed the work of his hands, so that his flocks and herds are spread throughout the land. But now stretch out your hand and strike everything he has, and he will surely curse you to your face." The Lord said to Satan, "Very well, then, everything he has is in your power, but on the man himself do not lay a finger." Then Satan went out from the presence of the Lord. (Job 1:6-12 NIV)

In Job 1:13-19, Job lost his oxen, donkeys, camels, servants to thieves and his sheep to fire. Then, a mighty wind collapsed on his children's house and killed all of them.

JOB's **FEAR** OF GOD

Forsake

Evil

When his health deteriorated, and the temptation to doubt God's justice came, Job chose to forsake evil. "His wife said to him, "Are you still maintaining your integrity? Curse God and die!" He replied, "You are talking like a foolish woman. Shall we accept good from God, and not trouble?" In all this, Job did not sin in what he said" (Job 2:9,10 NIV). His wife chose NOT to grow as a Proverbs 31 woman of valor at that moment.

Acknowledge God in every situation

When Job struggled with his sickness, questions, and friends who tempted him to doubt God's presence, Job bravely chose to acknowledge God. "I know that my redeemer lives, and that in the end he will stand on the earth" (Job 19:25 NIV). He also answered with one of my favorite Bible verses, "But he knows the way that I take; when he has tested me, I will come forth as gold" (Job 23:10 NIV).

Reverence/Worship the Lord with all our hearts

Job faced the temptation to doubt God's sovereignty and goodness. Instead, he said, "Naked I came from my mother's womb, and naked I will depart. The Lord gave and the Lord has taken away; may the name of the Lord be praised" (Job 1:21 NIV).

Job shines forth as an example of a maturing 'fear of God' heart.

- He **Forsook Evil** as it came to him in various forms.
- He **Acknowledged God's almighty attributes,**

  instead of wallowing in his struggles.
- He **Reverenced and worshiped** His Redeemer and Guide

Light Year

By David Gentry Thompson

God spoke it, and it was

Cause 168,000 miles is a long way to travel from the center of all universes

Christ the Center and the Circumference of absolutely everything

I keep closing my eyes and hoping the stars of the night will start to shoot

when I break free from eternity and start time

It's all mine

We find an abundance of days, the minutes tick by with certain pain and

pleasure, questions…is there a plan? Four laws?

Call me blind, tell me signs, again one breath and it was

Senses wrapped around a haughty moment, spirits enraptured

like archangels at flight over the waters of the seas

Sunday…oh Sunday, come

Evil is real; science is a mess, faith flickers with the force of a shuttle headed

into the sky…sometimes we find a trillion and its start to climb

One million in one: oh sun, come

A moment of silence in a vast ocean of time and space,

comes to the fulcrum of one precious scarred face.

"For God, who said, 'Let light shine out of darkness,' has shone in our hearts to

give the light of the knowledge of the glory of God in the face of Jesus Christ."

2 Corinthians 4:6 (NIV)

3. Growing Fear of God Roots

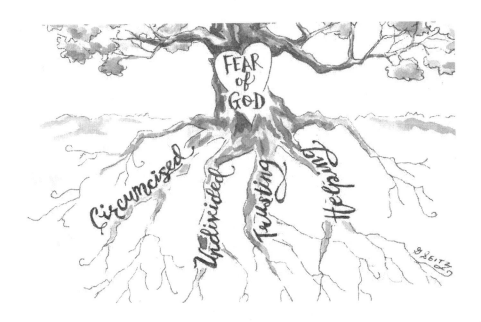

After looking into the heart of the 'fear of God,' we know how it is defined, developed, and embodied in a person like Job. Next, we are going to focus on the 'fear of God' Scriptures that visualize the roots that anchor the woman of valor. In my study of these verses, I found they divided into four focused areas.

Fear of God Roots

1. Circumcised Heart—Humble

2. Undivided Heart—Wholehearted

3. Trusting Heart—Holding Fast

4. Helpful Heart—Helping

For this Growing 'Fear of God' Roots section, first, we will look at the 'Fear of God' Root Scriptures and let them speak to our hearts. Then, I will give summary points of each root, along with Personal Root Growth examples.

Root 1   Circumcised Heart—Humble

Deuteronomy 10:12-22

And now, Israel, what does the Lord your God ask of you but to **fear the Lord your God,** to walk in obedience to him, to love him, to serve the Lord your God with all your heart and with all your soul, 13 and to observe the Lord's commands and decrees that I am giving you today for your own good? 14 To the Lord your God belong the heavens, even the highest heavens, the earth and everything in it. 15 Yet the Lord set his affection on your ancestors and loved them, and he chose you, their descendants, above all the nations—as it is today.

16 **Circumcise your hearts,** therefore, and **do not be stiff-necked any longer.** 17 For the Lord your God is God of gods and Lord of lords, the great God, mighty and awesome, who shows no partiality and accepts no bribes. 18 He defends the cause of the fatherless and the widow, and loves the foreigner residing among you, giving them food and clothing. 19 And you are to love those who are foreigners, for you yourselves were foreigners in Egypt.

20 **Fear the Lord your God and serve him.** Hold fast to him and take your oaths in his name. 21 He is the one you praise; he is your God, who performed for you those great and awesome wonders you saw with your own eyes. 22 Your ancestors who went down into Egypt were seventy in all, and now the Lord your God has made you as numerous as the stars in the sky." (NIV)

Characteristics of Circumcised Heart Root

- Seeks to cut away old sins and become sensitive to the Lord
- Not stiff-necked or resistant to the Lord
- Empathy toward others in need
- Desires to hold fast to the Lord

Colossians 2:9-13

For in Christ all the fullness of the Deity lives in bodily form, 10 and in Christ you have been brought to fullness. He is the head over every power and authority. 11 **In him you were also circumcised with a circumcision not performed by human hands. Your whole self ruled by the flesh was put off when you were circumcised by Christ,** 12 having been buried with him in baptism, in which you were also raised with him through your faith in the working of God, who raised him from the dead. 13 When you were dead in your sins and in the uncircumcision of your flesh, God made you alive with Christ. He forgave us all our sins. (NIV)

Characteristics of Circumcised Heart Root

- Brought to the fullness of Christ as He cuts away our old self
- Buried and raised in Christ through faith in the working of God
- Alive with Christ and forgiven of all our sins

Jeremiah 4:1-4

"If you, Israel, will return, then return to me," declares the Lord. "If you put your detestable idols out of my sight and no longer go astray,
2 and if in a truthful, just and righteous way you swear, 'As surely as the Lord lives,' then the nations will invoke blessings by him and in him they will boast."
3 This is what the Lord says to the people of Judah and to Jerusalem: "Break up your unplowed ground and do not sow among thorns.
4 **Circumcise yourselves to the Lord, circumcise your hearts,** you people of Judah and inhabitants of Jerusalem, or my wrath will flare up and burn like fire because of the evil you have done—burn with no one to quench it." (NIV)

Characteristics of Circumcised Heart Root

- Returns to the Lord and puts away detestable idols
- Lives in submission to the Lord
- Breaks up hard areas and does not sow among thorns
- Cuts away from her life what God hates

Summary of the Circumcised Heart—Humble Heart

The first step in fearing God is to recognize that He is Lord of all. After we accept Christ's sacrifice for our sin, we must continue to allow God to do his pruning work in our hearts to grow deep roots. Historically, the purpose of the circumcision of Jewish baby boys was to identify them with the true people of God. God's cutting work in our lives is evidence that we belong to Him.

Root Growth Journal

Pain is usually part of the cutting work of the Divine Pruner seeking to deepen our roots. The pain that helps us grow spiritually often comes from physical, mental, or emotional realms. Physical pain is something I like to avoid. As a child and young adult, I was healthy and active. During our engagement, I came down with an unclear condition of total exhaustion. With the help of my mother, I was able to prepare for the wedding. I rested and provided the plan, while she exerted all the energy. Living the first year of our marriage exhausted was a pruning process for my mind and heart. Thankfully, after a year my energy started to return. Several years later that condition was called chronic fatigue syndrome.

The Circumcised Heart that took root in me during those days of weariness was to grow in humility before the Lord taught in Deuteronomy 10. The chronic fatigue path the Lord chose befuddled me. He was showing me to accept my health issues with humility and not harden my heart with resentment. By the way, Rick's heart roots had many opportunities to grow while serving his new weary wife.

Our first child was born a year after the fatigue ended. During our maternity course, we learned that C-section delivers one out of ten babies. I was that 'one' each time as our three wonderful children enter the world.

I'm glad that the Lord did not inform me that surgery would be His preferred root deepening path for me. Including the three C-sections, my ten surgeries have nurtured humility and courage in me. Each time I prepared for the anesthesia, a renewed humility came over me, as I surrendered into the hands of the surgeon. I'm thankful that all the surgeries went well, but each came with a purpose along with the pain.

- Three brought the **joy** of new babies
- Two brought the **joy** of renewed eyesight, but I started having severe migraine **pain.** After four years, the Lord led us to a doctor, who found a sealed off sinus infection inside a cavity under my eye.
- Sinus surgery **removed** the infection causing the four years of **pain**
- Two parts of the thyroid gland **removed** the possibility of **cancer**
- One hernia repair needed after the **joy** of having three C-sections
- One gall bladder surgery **removed the intense pain** from gallstones

Believe me!! More than once I prayed for another way to have these physical issues resolved. As any surgeon knows, cutting is the only way at times to provide healing and a safe journey ahead. Our Lord is the Divine Surgeon. He alone knows our hearts, and how to fashion them, so they Forsake Evil, Acknowledge and Reverence Him. Through the cutting pain, His loving purpose is to create a woman of valor. *The Pulpit Commentary* speaks about the cutting involved with the circumcised root.

"God wants us to understand His hatred of sin. He wants us to loathe and abhor it with our whole heart. Our understanding of this happens when we go beyond the instinctive dislike for pain and the cutting that follows sin, instead of the hatred of sin itself. We should not just fear pain, but willingly let God heal our hearts."

I have seen God cut away at my spiritual heart to produce roots more than once in relationships, goals, health, and more. The Lord faithfully prunes our lives as John 15:2b describes, "every branch that does bear fruit He prunes, that it may bear more fruit."

Reflective Questions on the Circumcised Root

1. What insights came to mind about your Circumcised Root growth?

2. In what ways do you need to offer your heart and pray, "Lord, prune the needed areas of my life that I might become your rooted and fruitful woman of valor"?

3. Take a few minutes and jot down how you tend to resist the Lord's Divine Surgeon role in your life?

Root 2   Undivided Heart—Wholehearted

Psalm 86:11-12

Teach me your way, Lord, that I may rely on your faithfulness;
give me an **undivided heart that I may fear your name.**
I will praise you, Lord my God, with all my heart;
I will glorify your name forever. (NIV)

Characteristics of Undivided Heart Root

- Asks God to be taught how to rely on His faithfulness
- Prays to be undivided and to fear His name
- Praises and glorifies God wholeheartedly

Deuteronomy 13:1-4

If a prophet, or one who foretells by dreams, appears among you and announces to you a sign or wonder, 2 and if the sign or wonder spoken of takes place, and the prophet says, "Let us follow other gods" (gods you have not known) "and let us worship them," 3 you must not listen to the words of that prophet or dreamer. The Lord your **God is testing you to find out whether you love him with all your heart and with all your soul.** 4 It is the Lord your God you must follow, and him you must revere. Keep his commands and obey him; serve him and **hold fast to him.** (NIV)

Characteristics of Undivided Heart Root

- Tested to grow in love and loyalty toward God
- Follows and acknowledge only the true God
- Holds fast to God's commands and obeys them

Deuteronomy 17:14-20

When you enter the land the Lord your God is giving you and have taken possession of it and settled in it, and you say, "Let us set a king over us like all the nations around us," 15 be sure to **appoint over you a king the Lord your God chooses**. He must be from among your fellow Israelites. Do not place a foreigner over you, one who is not an Israelite. 16 The king, moreover, must not acquire great numbers of horses for himself or make the people return to Egypt to get more of them, for the Lord has told you, "You are not to go back that way again." 17 He must not take many wives, or his heart will be led astray. He must not accumulate large amounts of silver and gold.

18 **When he takes the throne of his kingdom, he is to write for himself on a scroll a copy of this law,** taken from that of the Levitical priests. 19 It is to be with him, and he is to read it all the days of his life so **that he may learn to revere the Lord his God and follow carefully all the words of this law and these decrees** 20 and not consider himself better than his fellow Israelites and turn from the law to the right or to the left. Then he and his descendants will reign a long time over his kingdom in Israel. (NIV)

Characteristics of Undivided Heart Root

- Wholeheartedly fears the Lord
- Wholehearted in following God's Word
- Humble before the Lord and how He leads others

Summary of the Undivided Heart

The undivided heart has one focus and one goal—
To love the Lord with all the heart, soul, and mind.

James 1:5-8

If any of you lacks wisdom, you should ask God, who gives generously to all without finding fault, and it will be given to you. 6 But when you ask, **you must believe and not doubt**, because the one who doubts is like a wave of the sea, blown and tossed by the wind. 7 That person should not expect to receive anything from the Lord. 8 Such a person is **double-minded and unstable in all they do**."(NIV)

The Undivided Heart Root provides stability as we grow as a woman of valor. To be rooted in the 'fear of God' with an undivided heart is to purpose to know God's Word and walk in His truth. When other voices call and beckon us to go down wrong paths, the **undivided heart** continues to commit itself to God and His ways. It means saying 'no' when others might not understand. The 'no' provides freedom to follow the Lord with our focus on His eternal goals and purposes.

Reflective Question on Undivided Heart Root

1. What areas of life do you find a struggle to have an undivided heart before the Lord?

2. How has the Lord given you an opportunity to be tested and grow in having an undivided heart toward Him?

Root 3. Trusting Heart—Holding Fast

Job 2:7-10

So Satan went out from the presence of the Lord and afflicted Job with painful sores from the soles of his feet to the crown of his head.

8 Then Job took a piece of broken pottery and scraped himself with it as he sat among the ashes. 9 His wife said to him, "Are you still maintaining your integrity? Curse God and die!"

10 He replied, "You are talking like a foolish woman."

"Shall we accept good from God, and not trouble?"

In all this, Job did not sin in what he said." (NIV)

Characteristics of Trusting Heart Root

- Accepts the good from God and trouble
- Maintains their integrity toward God when others try to make them doubt and curse God
- Believes in God's goodness, even in hard times

Psalm 33:18-22

But **the eyes of the Lord are on those who fear him, on those whose hope is in his unfailing love,** 19 to deliver them from death and keep them alive in famine. 20 We **wait in hope for the Lord;** he is our help and our shield. 21 In him our hearts rejoice, for **we trust in his holy name.** 22 May your unfailing love be with us, Lord, even as **we put our hope in you.** (NIV)

Characteristics of Trusting Heart Root

- Takes the hard times as opportunities to hope in God's unfailing love
- Waits in hope and trust in the Lord, not circumstances

Psalm 147:11

The Lord delights in **those who fear him,**
who put their hope in his unfailing love.

Characteristics of Trusting Heart Root

- Knows that God delights in those who trust Him
- Waits with hope in God's unfailing love

Summary of the Trusting Heart

James 1:2-4

Consider it pure joy, my brothers and sisters, whenever you face trials of many kinds, because you know that the testing of your faith produces perseverance. Let perseverance finish its work so that you may be mature and complete, not lacking anything." (NIV)

Perseverance is holding fast to the Lord as He finishes His work so we may mature. Such tenacity grows deep and strong roots. A young tree is unhindered by a great storm even though its roots are shallow. As the tree grows, its roots must push deep into the earth to tap the resources to produce abundant fruit and endure storms. In times of drought, a tree's roots will penetrate rock in quest of its needed resources. God allows droughts, trials and struggles to come our way so we will search for a more profound communion with Christ resulting in lasting fruit and real valor.

Quotes by C. S. Lewis on the Trusting Heart Root

"God has not been trying an experiment on my faith or love in order to find out their quality. He knew it already. It was I who didn't." from *Grief Observed.*

"We are not necessarily doubting that God will do the best for us; we are wondering how painful the best will turn out to be." from *God in the Dock.*

Root Growth Journal

In the early years of our ministry, we experienced some of the typical, but still challenging church issues. The gift of family and friends to process those befuddling days made trusting and holding fast more feasible. Nevertheless, it wasn't easy to see the purpose, besides being a hindrance to the ministry. As we look back on those days, we know that deep roots of trust developed in us while waiting on the Lord to answer prayer His way and in His time.

We had no idea that the Lord was preparing us for a new challenge and ministry. In 1992 we were called to go to Moscow, Russia as church planting missionaries. Our family grew in faith as we watched the Lord open doors and provide our financial and prayer support. He deepened our roots in our first ministry to provide maturity for us to physically uproot our family and begin ministering to a new culture. Our five years of pastoring Moscow Bible Church offered new growth pathways for trusting, undivided, and circumcised roots.

After being in our rented apartment less than a year, our Russian landlady came to our door and said she was moving in and wanted us to leave that night. Flabbergasted and frightened by her aggressive manner, we called a Russian Christian to come and translate for us. The facts were, we had no rights. Immediately, Natasha and her mother started moving into one of the three bedrooms with their portable beds. She was forcing us to move out as soon as possible! If the move only involved our family of five and suitcases, it might have seemed reasonable. Our challenge was to find a new apartment and move all our belongings; including beds, refrigerator, couches, bookcases and more. How would our family of elementary children accomplish this feat?

Two days later with the connections and efforts of Moscow Bible Church and the Campus Crusade for Christ staff, God showed our family how faithful, and worthy of our FEAR He is! A missionary gave us their study apartment to store everything. Amazingly, it was in our same large apartment complex with the same elevator. We moved everything in two days! Forty plus missionaries and Russian believers heard of our need and came non-stop to help us accomplish this exodus.

After all of our belongings were stored, our family walked to another believer's apartment to stay until we flew home for Christmas. On the way, our children said, "Wow! We have to write this story down and tell others how the Lord provided for our family through His people." Even as I type these words, tears trickle down my face as I think of how deep the 'fear of God' roots grew in all us during those challenging days. Not long ago, one of our sons said, "I measure the difficulty of my life situations based on that time in Russia when the impossible was made possible with God's faithful provision."

As parents, we could have feared the impact of that time on our family. Instead of fearing the situation, the Lord was calling us to 'fear Him' with trusting hearts that He would provide and grow roots of stability and valor for His glory. A year later, I needed my heart root at a deeper level when our oldest son had a skiing accident. Thankfully, friends and skilled doctors provided the immediate help needed to stitch the wound. As a mom, moments of fear and concern for our kids can cut deep into our hearts trying to sever our trust in the goodness of God. Our son's positive response to trust the Lord helped our family push forward.

My next root growing challenge was a four-year journey of migraine pain that started after I had early cataract surgery. Something about entering in and out of severe head pain without a correct diagnosis year after year became a new burrowing process for my heart. As I suffered, the Lord encouraged me through family, friends and His Word. Here is one of my 'root' proses.

Beauty in the Battle

As I endure the rages of another siege of sickness,
positivity of spirit seems incongruent.
Faith still believes but with Psalms of Lament,
Where, oh where is your Spirit, answers to prayer and needed shore of relief?
Then, an unexpected glance out the window,
On the barren Rose of Sharon bush have burst
the gorgeous periwinkle blossoms my eyes await each year.
My Lord calls to my weary soul, "I am here, I know the battles in life will
appear without cause. Roots take time to regather,
what I surge forth, to grow such beauty in your soul!

The Oak Tree

A mighty wind blew night and day

It stole the oak tree's leaves away

Then snapped its boughs and pulled its bark

Until the oak was tired and stark

But still, the oak tree held its ground

While other trees fell all around

The weary wind gave up and spoke,

"How can you still be standing, Oak?"

The oak tree said," I know that you

Can break each branch of mine in two,

Carry every leaf away,

Shake my limbs, and make me sway.

But I have roots stretched in the earth.

You'll never touch them, for you see,

They are the deepest part of me.

Until today, I wasn't sure

Of just how much I could endure.

But now I've found, with thanks to you,

I'm stronger than I ever knew.

Anonymous

Root 4   Helping Heart—Toward Others

Psalm 34:11-14

Come, my children, listen to me; **I will teach you the fear of the Lord.**
12 Whoever of you loves life and desires to see many good days,
13 keep your tongue from evil and your lips from telling lies.
14 **Turn from evil and do good; seek peace and pursue it.** (NIV)

Characteristics of Helping Heart Root

- Looks to the Lord to be taught the fear of God
- Relates to others in righteous ways
- Turns from evil and does good toward others
- Pursues peace with others

II Chronicles 19:4-9

Jehoshaphat lived in Jerusalem, and he went out again among the people from Beersheba to the hill country of Ephraim and **turned them back to the Lord,** the God of their ancestors. **5** He appointed judges in the land, in each of the fortified cities of Judah. **6** He told them, "Consider carefully what you do, because **you are not judging for mere mortals but for the Lord,** who is with you whenever you give a verdict.

7 Now let the fear of the Lord be on you. Judge carefully, for with the Lord our God there is no injustice or partiality or bribery." 8 In Jerusalem also, Jehoshaphat appointed some of the Levites, priests, and heads of Israelite families to **administer the law of the Lord** and to **settle disputes.** And they lived in Jerusalem. 9 He gave them these orders: **"You must serve faithfully and wholeheartedly in the fear of the Lord."** (NIV)

Characteristics of Helpful Heart Root

- Seeks to turn others back to the Lord
- Serves and judges carefully with fear of the Lord
- Leads others faithfully and wholeheartedly

Proverbs 8:12-13

I, wisdom, dwell together with prudence;
I possess knowledge and discretion.
To fear the Lord is to hate evil; I hate pride and arrogance, evil behavior and perverse speech. (NIV)

Characteristics of Helpful Heart Root

- Treats others with humility
- Chooses to not act with evil behavior
- Purposes to not use depraved or corrupt speech

Root Growth Journal

Deepening in the 'fear of God' requires a heart that believes God created humankind. Everyone is worthy of our helpful and righteous response as God's child. Sometimes that is not easy as we relate to others. When things do not go our way, are we more controlled by our disgust at what the person is doing or by the way the Lord wants me to handle the situation? Will I choose to act with humility, godly speech and behavior, as the Lord challenges me to grow a helpful heart root?

While we were still missionaries in Russia, we received word that my mother had a massive stroke during her back surgery. That type of news is hard to face, especially when you are a world away. Once again the Lord was seeking to root me in forsaking resentment and acknowledging that He would be faithful. Thankfully, my mother lived, but with many limitations that affected her personality. The mom and grandmother we had vacationed with the year before was no longer the energetic, serving person we knew. The stroke had impacted part of her brain that made her organizational skills and outgoing personality limited. Over the seventeen years that she lived in this different state, we all learned how to love her anew. For my sister and me, it was a long journey of grief. Our mom was one of the most helpful and loving people in our lives. It was our time to grow in the Helping Heart Root toward her.

Summary of Helping Heart

As we desire to bear fruit in every good work, we are challenged in Revelation 2:9-10 (NIV).

> "I know your afflictions and your poverty,
> yet you are rich...Do not be afraid of what you are
> about to suffer...be faithful, even to the point of death
> and I will give you life as your victor's crown." (NIV)

The helping heart is deeply anchored in the fruitfulness of our woman of valor. As she gives to her family and world, she knows her rewards come from God.

The Circumcised, Undivided, Trusting and Helping Heart Roots will continue to grow anchoring our lives and bearing fruit as we live as a woman of valor, who has a 'fear of God' heart.

Forsaking
Evil
Acknowledging God in every circumstance
Reverencing the Lord with a heart of worship

In Isaiah 11:1-5 we see the heavenly example of the 'fear of God' in a prophecy concerning Christ's coming to earth. He is the source of every Rooted Woman of Valor.

Our Heavenly Example of the Fear God

Isaiah 11:1-5

an amazing prophecy

about Jesus concerning

the **fear of the Lord.**

A shoot will come up from the stump of Jesse;

From his roots a Branch will bear fruit.

2 The Spirit of the Lord will rest on him—

the Spirit of wisdom and of understanding,

the Spirit of counsel and of might,

the Spirit of the knowledge and fear of the Lord—

3 **and he will delight in the fear of the Lord.**

He will not judge by what he sees with his eyes,

or decide by what he hears with his ears;

4 but with righteousness he will judge the needy,

with justice he will give decisions for the poor of the earth.

He will strike the earth with the rod of his mouth;

with the breath of his lips he will slay the wicked.

5 Righteousness will be his belt

and faithfulness the sash around his waist. (NIV)

Reflective Root Questions

1. Evaluate your understanding and application of the 'fear of God'.
Take the time to explain it to someone else.

F

E

A

R

2. What stage are you at in your understanding of the 'fear of God?'

3. Take each Heart Root and ask the Lord what He might be saying to
you and your heart. How is each root growing deeper in your life?
Circumcised

Undivided

Trusting

Helping

4. Take time and commune with your Lord, the Spirit of wisdom,
understanding, counsel, might, and valor! Isaiah 11:2

A tree does not grow itself.
It grows in response to certain stimuli
or specific conditions which surround it.

Roots are surrounded by soil.

The vigor, quality, and strength
of a tree is determined
by the mineral content of the soil.

In the spiritual realm the strength
and stamina of my character will depend
upon where I choose to sink
my spiritual roots
and feed my mind, heart, and soul.

As A Tree Grows by Philip Keller

Soil Factor

of the

Woman of Valor

Soil Factor of Woman of Valor

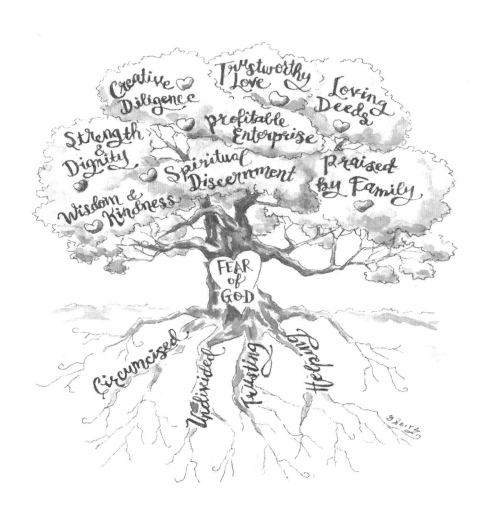

Rooted Woman of Valor

Our Rooted Woman of Valor tree is complete with her crown full of fruitful character and her 'fear of God' heart growing deep roots. Now we turn our search to the soil and resources that surround her roots and provide the nutrients for her to develop strength and vigor.

Jeremiah 17:7-8 paints the portrait of the soil and resources for our roots.

> Blessed is the one who trusts in the Lord,
> whose confidence is in him.
> They will be like **a tree planted by the water**
> that **sends out its roots by the stream**.
> It **does not fear** when heat comes;
> its leaves are always green.
> It **has no worries** in a year of drought
> and **never fails to bear fruit**. (NIV)

In his book, *As A Tree Grows*, Philip Keller, a specialist in the science of soil and production of crops, explains, "The best growth of a tree comes from adding the annual growth ring quietly without fanfare or frustration. We need to keep in mind that we grow by a continuous response to external stimuli. The great tasks of the roots' underground network are not only to anchor the tree to the ground, but much more important searching out and absorbing the available nutrients in the soil. The nutrients are taken up into the tree and built into the very fibers and tissues of the trunk and branches. This gives strength and sturdiness to the entire tree."

Soil Factor Questions

- How do I keep the soil of my life in good condition so that the 'fear of God' roots can grow deep?

- What waters the roots of my heart?

- What elements (minerals and humus) do I need to gather around my roots so they can draw in rich nutrients to grow consistently and richly?

1. Scriptural Resources for Spiritual Growth

The Scriptures provide ample guidance for nurturing the soil of our heart roots to produce abundant fruit.

Matthew 13:23

But the seed falling on **good soil** refers to someone who **hears the word and understands it.** This is the one who **produces a crop,** yielding a hundred, sixty or thirty times what was sown. (NIV)

Soil—Heart Plowed and Purified

Jeremiah 4:3,4

This is what the Lord says to the people of Judah and to Jerusalem: **Break up your unplowed ground** and **do not sow among thorns. Circumcise yourselves to the Lord, circumcise your hearts,** you people of Judah and inhabitants of Jerusalem, or my wrath will flare up and burn like fire because of the evil you have done, burn with no one to quench it. (NIV)

The soil around our hearts needs regular plowing. We need to open our hearts to the Lord in hard areas that we tend to resist. The passage warns us not to sow thorns which will only hinder and block the growth of our fruitfulness. Instead, we need to ask God to help us purify the soil of our life—clean out anything in our body or spirit that hinders growth.

II Corinthians 7:1

Therefore, since we have these promises, dear friends, **let us purify ourselves from everything that contaminates body and spirit, perfecting holiness out of reverence (fear) for God.** (NIV)

The challenge is to purify the soil around our **FEAR** of God-heart roots by:

- **F**orsaking (purify ourselves)
- **E**vil (everything that contaminates body and spirit.)
- **A**cknowledge God (perfecting holiness)
- **R**everence (worship God)

Real Joy

Lyrics by Tiffany Danae Thompson

From *One Voice* album

I feel the floodgate; I feel my floodgate open

The healing water, the sweetest water starting to flow

I see the breakers; I see my breakers are crumbling

The mighty river, the holy river coming home

Bringing joy, real joy

Underlining and overwhelming over me

It is in the quiet; it's in the quiet that I hear

Words so deep, truths so deep doesn't disappear.

I sense a smile; I sense a smile in the still

The Spirit's moving, healing, restoring a broken world

Bringing joy, real joy, underlining and overwhelming over me.

I found life at the cross, turn around and pour it out.

I found love in Christ, now turn around pour it out.

Sharing joy real joy, underlining and overwhelming,

Joy, real joy, it's underlining and overwhelming

Underlining and overwhelming over me

Water—Intake of God's Word

Along with rich and plowed soil, our Heart Roots need to have a steady stream of living water from God's Word.

Psalm 1:2,3

But whose delight is in the law of the Lord, and who meditates on his law day and night. That person is like a tree planted by **streams of water,** which yields its fruit in season and whose leaf does not wither—whatever they do prospers. (NIV)

John 7:37

Jesus said, "Let anyone who is thirsty come to me and drink. Whoever believes in Me, as Scripture has said, **rivers of living water will flow from within them.**"(NIV)

"Vital life processes of living things depends on the moisture in its cell. Water is essential to survival, determining its health and vigor. A flourishing tree is 80% moisture, thus water spells the difference of desert to forest," states Philip Keller in his book, *As A Tree Grows.*

Having well-watered soil for our heart roots involves drinking in God's Word. We'll develop rich and well-watered roots for the seasons of our life, as we delight in the reading, studying, and applying of God's Word. As I review my annual life rings, I see my intake of God's Word varies. Whether single, married, mother, or empty nester the seasons of our lives change. We can expect the amount of time we have to drink in God's Word to vary also. The key is to delight in God's Word and seek to be planted by His streams throughout our lives.

Along with weekly sermons, Bible studies, and Christian music, my preferred method for soaking in God's Word has been to take one book of the Bible for a month or more. I have journals from the years of my insights, applications, and prayers. Some days I had time for a glance at one verse. Other days there was time to study and make notes. By focusing on one book of the Bible, I have come to know, remember, and teach from specific books.

For me, it provides a natural outflow for meditation and choosing meaningful Bible verses to memorize and pray. The key is to select the variety of learning and growing style that fits you.

This book comes out of several months of reading, journaling, and applying the book of Proverbs to my life. By the time I reached Proverbs 31, I wanted to read it slowly and cross-reference verses. Then, I came to the verse, "but a woman who fears the Lord is to be praised. Honor her for all her hands have done." I decided to take the time to do a word/phrase study of 'fear of God.' The long reflection and study impacted me so much that I turned it into a women's retreat and this book.

As I review other quiet time journals, they remind me of verses or chapters that watered my heart roots. As I made life decisions, parented, ministered, and sought to be wise in relating to other, the Lord used His Word to counsel my heart and mind. As Psalm 119:24 says, "Your statutes are my delight, they are my counselors." The longest chapter of the Bible's bottom-line!

Being a grandmother reminds me how busy raising children can be. We often feel like there is not enough time or brain space to be watered by God's Word. As a grandparent or parent, it is a sweet time to water our little growing plants with living water! Nothing like a captive audience, to sing Scripture songs, to read Bible stories, and to teach them to pray. When they express their delight at a new Bible story, I see Psalm 1:2,3, "delight in the law of the Lord...like a tree planted by streams of water," begin to take root in their hearts.

Water is the crucial resource that carries the elements through the soil for the growth of a tree. As we keep our hearts open to the Lord by seeking to plow the ground of our heart, we need to take time to absorb the water of God's Word.

One Voice

By Tiffany Danae Thompson
From *One Voice* album

I'm listening for Your heartbeat,

but it's noisy on this city street

I'm searching for open doors,

but bright lights keep blinding me

I fall to the ground with empty hands

I long for the sound, so come on in

Call me in

One Voice, One Voice is all I want,

all I want to hear

Is Your voice, Your voice loud and clear

Would I miss it if I fell asleep?

Would I notice it if it rang through my dreams?

But if You were to pass me by, would I even recognize?

I fall to the ground with empty hands,

I long for the sound, so call me in, call me in

If You breathe, I'm listening

If You speak, I'm listening

Yes…loud and clear

Air and Minerals—Connection through Prayer

John 15:7

If you remain in me and my words remain in you, **ask whatever you wish**, and it will be done for you. (NIV)

John 14:15-17a

If you love me, keep my commands. And I will ask the Father, and He will **give you another advocate to help you** and be with you forever--the Spirit of truth. (NIV)

Ezekiel 47:12

Fruit trees of all kinds will grow on both banks of the river. Their leaves will not wither, nor will their fruit fail. **Every month they will bear fruit, because the water from the sanctuary flows to them.** Their fruit will serve for food and their leaves for healing. (NIV)

As we interact with the Lord in prayer, the Spirit moves in our hearts and causes us to continue to grow as a His woman of valor. My favorite prayer resource through the years is *Face to Face: Praying the Scriptures for Spiritual Growth* by Kenneth Boa. It is a daily guide to pray Scripture based on the principles that Jesus gave us in the Lord's Prayer of Matthew 6:

Adoration, Confession,
Renewal, Petition,
Intercession, Affirmation
and Thanksgiving.

As a prayer resource, it provides the blend of reading verses of Scripture with prayer and watering my soul's soil more richly. Having a prayer partner or small group to share our spiritual journey in prayer and the Word is a great resource. In Matthew 18:20, Jesus promises, "For where two or three are gathered in my name, there am I among them."

The Teaching

By Derick Gentry Thompson
From **Rock Gospel of Jesus Christ** album

Our Father in Heaven
Holy with perfection
Christ the Son of God
Through prayer man's only connection
What is unseen
Is more vivid

Hallowed be Thy Name
Kingdom come,
Will be done
On earth as in Heaven

Faith takes form in the supplication
Patience always strengthens
A waning spirit
Belief is clearer in the realization
What is unseen
Is more vivid

Give us our bread
Grace to forgive
Strength in temptation
Ask, and you shall receive
Seek, and you shall find
Knock, and you will be ushered in

Ask, and you shall receive
Seek, and you shall find
Knock, and you will be ushered in
Solitude amplifies a whisper

2. Fear of God Heart Roots and Spiritual Disciplines

Definition of Spiritual Disciplines

"Spiritual Disciplines are an activity undertaken to bring us into more effective cooperation with Christ and His Kingdom," states Dallas Willard in his book, *Spirit of the Disciplines*.

- Inward—Word of God--read, listen, study, memorize, journal, prayer (adoration, confession, thanksgiving and supplication) worship-meditation, singing
- Outward—Service to others, giving of resources, talent, time
- Corporate—Worship, communion, confession, discipleship

Watering and plowing up of our soul's soil is important for our 'Fear of God' Heart Roots to spur spiritual growth.

Each 'Fear of God' Heart Root is nurtured by one spiritual discipline:

Circumcised Heart (Humble)	Confession to the Lord
Undivided Heart (Wholehearted)	Commitment to the Word
Trusting Heart (Holding Fast)	Commitment to Prayer
Helping Heart (Helping others)	Commitment to Fellowship
	& Witnessing

Celebration of Discipline by Richard Foster brings out an important growth process as we seek to develop roots deeply resourced by God's Word, prayer, fellowship, and witnessing. "Spiritual disciplines are an inward and spiritual reality, and the inner attitude of the heart is far more crucial than the mechanics of reading Scripture, Bible study, prayer, etc.—for coming into the reality of the spiritual life."

Colossians 2:6,7

So then, just as you received Christ Jesus as Lord, continue to live in Him, **rooted and built up in Him,** strengthened in the faith as you were taught and overflowing with thankfulness. (NIV)

While staying at our home, our niece, Ashley, started planting carrot seeds in clear jars with paper towels to hold the seeds and water in place. After many days the seeds burst forth into little seedlings. Only consistent contact with water, air, soil, and minerals will develop such a minuscule sprout of green to the crunchy carrot we enjoy. God alone can bring forth such fruitfulness in our lives, as we assist Him in the nurture of our soul.

Let's look at the benefits of spiritual disciplines as we keep the soil of our heart roots primed for growth.

Benefits of Spiritual Disciplines

I Timothy 4:7,8

Have nothing to do with godless myths and old wives' tales; rather, **train yourself to be godly.** For physical training is of some value, but **godliness has value for all things, holding promise for both the present life and the life to come.** (NIV)

Philippians 2:12

Therefore, my dear friends, as you have always obeyed—not only in my presence, but now much more in my absence—**continue to work out your salvation with fear and trembling.** (NIV)

Summary of Spiritual Disciplines

Richard Foster explains, "The farmer is helpless to grow grain—all he can do is provide the right conditions for the growing process." The Spiritual Disciplines are the means in which we can keep the soil of our lives prepared for growth.

A special joy is in all love for objects we revere,
Thus joy in God will always be proportioned to our fear.
The dread to miss such love as Thine,
Makes fear but love's excess.

Frederick W. Faber

Jan's Soil Insight

- The goal of spiritual disciplines in the Word and prayer provides the resources we need to nourish the various seasons of our lives. My young mom 'motto' was, "Spend time in prayer and the Word on the move or when you can."

- Choose one book of the Bible and walk through it slowly, spoonful by spoonful. Plan 10-15 minutes each day to soak up one truth for prayer and wisdom to live that day.

- Journal one truth you are drinking in each day or week. Turn it into a prayer request for you, your family, children, or others. Let that verse or insight be your central prayer that week. Take time to review your focused verse(s) once a month to reflect on how God is making you into a woman of valor.

Often poems and songs are used by the Lord to speak to my heart and nurture the richness of the soil of my soul. Our daughter, Tiffany Thompson, wrote the following lyrics. She rooted this song in Psalm 42 written by King David, who longed for His God to be near and meet his needs.

Waterfall Embrace

By Tiffany Danae Thompson
No gloss,
No sheen,
Standing in the space between
No hurt
No pain
Shelters me from your grace
Just you
With me
Light from you is my remedy
Just you
With me
Mending parts no one else can see

Being with you
I touch the still point
Of a tilting, turning world
Deep are my longings
But deeper your calling
A waterfall embrace of love

Drown me
In silence
If it means I can feel your kiss
Golden
Glimpses
Light up life like a birthday wish
Just you
With me
Turn time into a remedy
Just you
With me
Mending parts no one else can see

Conclusion

Who can find a woman of valor, an excellent wife? Proverbs 31:10

The answer to that Proverbs 31 question was the quest of this book. We took time to dig into the twenty-two alphabetical and inspired verses the queen gave her son as a vision for his future wife. At first glance, this woman of valor appears to be an ordinary, busy woman at work in her home and world. The vision of her Fruit Factor became evident in her courageous attitudes in everyday actions. Trustworthy Love, Creative Diligence, Profitable Enterprise, Loving Deeds and Character in her Spirit of Strength and Dignity, her Eyes of Spiritual Discernment and her Mouth of Wisdom and Kindness burst forth as the harvest of her life realms. The impact of her fruit factor produced her children rising to call her blessed, along with her husband and his praise.

This woman of valor and character is our Heavenly King's vision for each of us. Graciously, He doesn't ask us to read these verses and achieve them in our strength. Proverbs 31:30 reveals the secret source of her fruitfulness.

**Charm is deceitful, and beauty is vain,
but a woman who fears the Lord is to be praised.**

The queen clarifies that a charming personality or outside beauty should never be the heart of this quest. Digging below her surface to the Root Factor provides insight into her secret source, "but a woman who fears the Lord is to be praised."

The Fear Factor of her life reveals a heart that understands the 'fear of God.' Our woman of valor is brave and fearless because she has moved from being self-focused to God-focused. She agrees with God about her sin and has found refuge in the death and resurrection of Jesus Christ, as God's provision. The fruit of her actions and attitudes are rooted in Him as she grows in "bearing fruit in every good work and increasing in the knowledge of God, being strengthened with all power according to His glorious might" (Colossians 1:11).

She enjoys the benefits of 'fearing God' but knows that He expects her to live a life of **Forsaking Evil, Acknowledging, and Reverencing Him as her Lord.** Her 'Fear of God' heart roots deepen through obedience, as she weathers the challenges God brings to produce in her a Circumcised, Undivided, Trusting, and Helping heart. She knows that Christ is her Heavenly example, "His roots will bear fruit...and He will delight in the fear of the Lord." (Isaiah 11:1-3)

Her Soil Factor bases itself in Scriptures like Psalm 1 and Jeremiah 17. Her vision is to be a strong tree planted by the water of God's Word. As she seeks to acknowledge and reverence the Lord, her soil grows in richness by prayer, obedience, and abiding in Christ and His Word.

Job, the man who feared God, understood that his roots needed to be surrounded by eternal soil to feed his soul.

> **But he knows the way that I take; when He has tested me,**
> **I will come forth as gold.**
> **My feet have closely followed His steps;**
> **I have not departed from the commands of His lips;**
> **I have treasured the words of His mouth more than my daily**
> **bread.** (Job 23:10-12)

May these words of Job be your prayer as you offer the Fruit, Root, and Soil Factors of your life before the Lord to grow as...

His Rooted Woman of Valor.

Amen

Notes for Rooted Woman of Valor

Fruit Factor of Woman of Valor

- Hom, Exell, Spence, *The Pulpit Commentary* (Peabody, MA: Hendrickson Publishers, 1985), http://biblehub.com/commentaries/pulpit/proverbs/31.htm.
- Scharlotte Rich, *Growing by Heart* (Colorado Springs, CO: NavPress, 2004).
- Max Lucado, *Traveling Light* (Nashville, TN: Thomas Nelson, 2006).
- Rachel Held Evans, "3 Things You Might Not Know about Proverbs 31," RachelHeldEvans.com, May 12, 2014, http://rachelheldevans.com/blog/3-things-you-might-not-know-about-proverbs-31 (accessed April 2017).
- Joyce Kilmer, *Trees and Other Poems* (CreateSpace Independent Publishing Platform, 2016).
- Tony Evans, *Kingdom Woman: Embracing Your Purpose, Power ,and Possibilitie* (Wheaton, IL: Tyndale House, 2015).
- Ulrich Schaffer, "Walking Past My Sleeping Children," from *The Love of the Children* (NYC, NY: Harper & Row, First Edition edition, 1980).
- Elisabeth Elliot, *Through Gates of Splendor* (Grand Rapids, MI: Baker Books-Spire Books, 1970).
- Paul Lee Tan, *Encyclopedia of 7700 Illustration: Signs of the Times* (TN: Assurance Publishers, 1990), The Power of Word-Illustration #6380.
- Rabbi Yosef Tropper, *The Aishes Chayil Song* (America: www.YosefTropper.com, 2014).
- OJB is the Orthodox Jewish Bible.

Root Factor of Woman of Valor

- C. S. Lewis, *Grief Observed,* (NYC, NY: Harper & Row, 1961).
- C. S. Lewis, *God in the Dock,* (Grand Rapids, MI: Wm. B. Eerdmans Publishing Co.,1970).
- Pat Palau, *Scared to Death* (UK: Monarch Books, 2008).
- Derick Gentry Thompson, "A Situation," lyrics, singer-songwriter, Story Before album, (Chicago, IL,2007).
- Derick Gentry Thompson, "Overture," lyrics, singer-songwriter, Rock Gospel of Jesus Christ album (Chicago, IL, 2005).
- David Gentry Thompson, "Lightyear," poet, (Boone, NC, 2014).

Soil Factor of Woman of Valor

- Dallas Willard, *Spirit of Disciplines* (New York: HarperCollins, 1998).
- Catherine McNiel, *Long Days of Small Things: Motherhood as a Spiritual Discipline* (Colorado Springs, CO: NavPress, 2017).
- Richard Foster, *Celebration of Discipline* (New York: HarperCollins, 1998).
- Gary Thomas, *Sacred Pathways: Discover Your Soul's Path to God* (Grand Rapids, MI: Zondervan, 1996).
- Derick Gentry Thompson, "The Teaching," lyrics, singer-songwriter, *Rock Gospel of Jesus Christ* album (Chicago, IL, 2005).
- Tiffany Danae Thompson, "Real Joy," lyrics, singer-songwriter, *One Voice* album on iTunes under Tiffany Thompson (Wash. DC, 2012).
- Tiffany Danae Thompson, "One Voice," lyrics, singer-songwriter, *One Voice* album on iTunes under Tiffany Thompson (Wash. DC, 2012).
- W. Phillip Keller, *As a Tree Grows* (Grand Rapids, MI: Fleming H Revell, 1966).
- Tiffany Danae Thompson, "Waterfall," singer-songwriter on iTunes under Tiffany Thompson and Danae (NYC, NY, 2017).

Contact Information

This material is also available for presentation in message or retreat format.

To purchase additional copies buy on Amazon.com.

For more information contact:

Jan C. Thompson

Email: jancthompson@gmail.com

Blog: jancthompson.com

Phone: 630-881-7050

Made in the USA
Lexington, KY
12 March 2018